FINCA

RENOVATING
AN OLD FARMHOUSE
IN SPAIN

Alec and Erna Fry

SANTANA
BOOKS

Acknowledgements

This fascinating project, and the book which arose from it, could never have been possible without the support of many who went out of their way to help us. So our thanks must go: to our son, Thomas, who configured our outdated laptop PC and mobile phone so that we were able to communicate with the world, independently of telephone lines and mains power, from the top of our mountain. To our UK neighbours Ian and Jenny, without whose help it would have been almost impossible to get away and undertake this project. To Kevin Sealey of Fincas Andalucía and Obracol Developments of Colmenar, and his wife Marilo Sealey and staff for their generous help, especially in compiling the glossary at the back of the book. To Elizabeth and John Sutherland-Hawes for sending us a regular photographic record of building progress while we were in the UK, and for rescuing us from an embarrassingly large number of scrapes of our own making; John was also kind enough to read through our manuscript and point out some of our more obvious blunders. To Ricardo Stutes of Beep (Torre del Mar), for his cheerful determination to connect us to Telefonica's internet service for mobiles, seemingly against all the odds, and for solving other computer-related problems. To the shopkeepers of Colmenar, for their patient attempts to make sense of our crudely illustrated shopping lists of hard-to-find oddments; and in particular to Jesús the grocer, one of the few to speak English, for answering so many questions and turning many of our shopping trips into informal Spanish lessons (and who else would have pursued our car quite so energetically down the road after we had inadvertently overpaid for our groceries?). To John the builder, for persevering with a difficult job despite our frequent interruptions, panic attacks and changes of heart, and to his wife Thelma for her local knowledge. To Juan, local garage owner, who continues to care for the battered 1988 hatchback which he supplied from the outset, sometimes using quite creative engineering techniques and paying little heed to normal working hours, and who has proved to be far removed from the pirata he once jokingly proclaimed himself to be. To Yves and Janet, and to John and Jodie, as it was our holidays in their delightful fincas which gave us the original idea. To the many interesting contributors to the Costa-del-Sol e-mail group, few of whom we have ever met, and especially to Louisa, Steve, Bill, Helen and Pete for their replies to our requests for information and advice.

Published May 2003 by Santana Books
Copyright © Alec and Erna Fry 2003
Designed by Andrea Carter

Finca – Renovating an old farmhouse in Spain
Is published by Ediciones Santana S.L.,
Apartado 422, Fuengirola 29640 (Málaga), Spain.
Tel. 952 485 838. Fax 952 485 367.
E-mail: info@santanabooks.com
www.santanabooks.com

Printed and bound in Spain by Gráficas San Pancracio S.L.,
Polígono Industrial San Luis, Málaga.

Depósito Legal: MA-639/2003
ISBN 84-89954-26-7.

Contents

... horse clump of prickly pear cactus, and ...

INTRODUCTION

When, after weeks of disappointment, we were shown around yet another remote, deserted farmhouse in the Málaga mountains in southern Spain on a rather chilly February day, we knew right away that this particular semi-ruin was destined to be our permanent holiday home of the future. It was in a quiet yet accessible spot, with spectacular views over the Málaga Mountains Natural Park to the west, to the sea beyond the mountain-top village of Comares to the south, and to the snow-capped Sierra mountains in the north-east. In short, it had everything—but it was a near-ruin.

Looking back, we can see now why the omens were too good to be ignored. Chosen in the year of our silver wedding anniversary, we fell in love with the place on St Valentine's Day. We wanted to call it Finca Valentin until we discovered from the Town Hall's plans that it was already named *Lagar de Corazones* (*Lagar* meaning a building where olives or wine is pressed and *Corazones*—hearts—being the name of the surrounding area).

Lagar de Corazones may have been chosen with our hearts but we were determined our heads would rule its restoration. Before going further, we took stock. Here we had an ancient and dilapidated farmhouse with a sagging roof, walls up to 85cm thick, no water, plumbing or drains, and a burned out electrical connection to a nearby pylon. There were three small inside rooms, a kitchen and fireplace with outside access only, an outside bread oven, a ripe-smelling mule stable, goat shed and pigsty.

Built into the side of a mountain, its only foundations being the solid rock beneath, it sloped so steeply that entering the next room uphill through each connecting door entailed climbing a minor staircase! Outside was a 3000 square metre plot with olive and almond trees, a huge clump of prickly pear cactus, and a eucalyptus tree which would provide welcome shade in summer.

How exactly should we set about restoring this unpromising cluster of assorted rooms to provide a comfortable holiday home—and maybe more—without destroying its character?

We had been DIY addicts for many years and done some occasional building work, but this was back home in the UK where we had worked with British materials and techniques: real solid bricks instead of flimsy things with holes in them; cement mortar instead of sun-baked mud and lime putty; roofs with rafters, battens and flat tiles instead of poles, bamboo and half-round tiles, a reliable supply of mains water and electricity; well-built roads for easy access, and a handy local builder's merchant who not only offered a quick, free delivery service but who spoke our language.

We had already been investigating techniques and materials used in Spain but now, with the purchase legalities under way, our research became urgent. Even though we had decided to use builders to do the basic structural work in our absence, rebuilding the sagging roofs and repairing those walls in danger of collapsing, we still wanted to understand what they were doing. This proved useful when problems arose and we had to make important decisions at the other end of an international telephone line.

The internet was an invaluable source of advice and information, and this book includes details of web sites, e-mailing lists and newsgroups that you can surf to your heart's content. More conventional sources proved just as useful. Open-Air Museums, historic building restoration societies, and standard works of reference all contained important information on the subject. But, in the final resort, nothing proved as effective as hands-on experience at the finca, starting in a small way on less important outbuildings before progressing to the main structure.

This book is the result of that experience. It is not a definitive building manual (most finca buyers in any case will place the major work in the hands of local builders) but it will help you understand just what your builder is doing and enable you to make informed decisions. It is the book we wish we could have read before we started buying and restoring our own finca. It would have saved us a great deal of time and money, though we must admit it was fun finding out the hard way.

Meet us on the Fincabook website.

If you need further help, if you would like to make a suggestion for improving future editions of this book, or if you have experiences of your own that you'd like to share with others, you can log on to our fincabook website: www.fincabook.com. In it you'll find further background details and updated photographs of our own restoration. With new products and services arriving all the time, the website will include more information on these. In fact it's rather like the DVD version of a film, and it contains all sorts of extra information that was squeezed out of the book, either from lack of space or because it would have needed frequent updating. The website includes a comprehensive list of links to other sites concerned with local information, property sales and restoration technicalities, and even explains how you can visit Colmenar and surrounding areas, sampling local village life for yourself and meeting property agents and builders. It will also link you to a bulletin board, through which may be able to make contact with other people renovating fincas in your chosen location. It may even be possible to arrange some get-togethers and demonstrations in due course.

CHAPTER 1

WHAT IS A FINCA?

Basic definitions. The history of the finca. Detective work on old properties. Lagares. Fincas don't suit everyone: the pros and cons. Village houses. The importance of the village.

Basic definitions

The Spanish term *finca*—or more correctly *finca rustica*—means a country property or farm with or without a house on it, but for most people the term conjures up a vision of a small farmhouse or *casa de campo* on a sizeable plot of land with fruit trees. This term can vary from region to region and elsewhere you'll come across other names such as *caserío, hórreo, masía, casona, pazo* and *barraca*.

In fact, some of the smaller buildings now being bought up eagerly for restoration were originally built as *casitas de apero* (agricultural tool sheds) and never intended or used for habitation. These will require extra work and expense in improving them up to the necessary standards of comfort and convenience.

In this book, when we say *finca* we are referring to the farmhouse or *cortijo* rather than the farmland. Within this meaning we include *molinos* (mills) and *lagares*, small country buildings where olives or grapes are pressed. The house we bought started out as a *lagar* (presumably for pressing grapes as the original press beam was discovered within the structure), but after almost three hundred years was converted to a farmhouse with an attached piggery, goathouse, mule stable and chicken house.

The Andalusian countryside is a delightful sight in early spring when even the bare mountainside around our finca becomes a mass of wild flowers.

History of the finca

The typical finca was solidly built out of local materials in such a way as to keep it cool in summer and warm in winter. While some of the smallest fincas might, even then, have been occupied on an occasional or seasonal basis, or even used mainly for storage, most of them would have been the farmer's main residence. Look out for clues like a well-used fireplace or cooking range, a well, animal quarters with feed troughs, an outside stone sink, an outside bread oven or separate kitchen with an entrance from outside, and worn-out, discarded cooking pots. Any of these features could point to regular use at some stage in its life.

Modern conveniences were unknown. Electricity was quite late in reaching even the smaller villages in Spain, let alone the campo.

Water would have come from the nearest well, carried by hand, or on the back of a donkey or mule; it would need to be close at hand if much livestock was being kept, and you may not need to look very far to discover its location. The kitchen fire was primarily used for cooking, with warmth during the cold winter evenings coming from the *mesa camilla*—a circular table with a pan of warm ashes below, with a heavy tablecloth which was draped across the laps of the occupants.

Mixed farming was the order of the day, and it is often still possible to work out where they would have kept the goats, pig, poultry and the mule according to the height of the built-in feed troughs. It was unusual to use separate, detached outbuildings for this purpose, the Spanish system being to build all animal shelters and sheds on to the house.

The chores of feeding and watering livestock under such basic conditions must have imposed a particularly heavy burden on the farmer and his wife. In fact, campo life was harsh and precarious, even in comparatively recent days, and the fact that it retains a small element of challenge is part of its attraction.

Detective work on an old finca

Many fincas underwent such changes over the years that it is not always easy to guess at their original layout. Most have been altered, added to, partly demolished, and rebuilt over time, often somewhat inexpertly by the farmer himself (and invariably without notifying the authorities, who would have taken little interest anyway in those days), for he would not have had the money to employ a builder.

Often the only way of determining the original boundary is by measuring the thickness of each wall. Originally, only two thicknesses would have been used—around 75-85cm for an outside wall, and rather less for any inside dividing walls or for the walls of animal quarters. You may also come across some lightweight internal dividing walls, sometimes stopping short of the ceiling, made from clay-covered bamboo canes. Mountain fincas would have been built straight on to the bedrock without any foundations whatever, but those in lower positions or on deeper soil may have the original simple footings that can still be traced, just below soil level.

If you need to lift and replace any floor tiles, you may well come across other clues to the original layout, for you may find signs of old walls or channels for carrying grape juice (as indeed we did). The layout of the finca varies according to local custom and building techniques, but there are certain common features. The very simplest and oldest buildings were often built with a single pitch to the roof, and if yours has a double pitch or ridge then you should consider the possibility that one entire side may have been added later.

Often the main building faces south, so that the eaves cast a shadow down over the doorway and window during the height of summer. The heavy main door would have been of solid timber, clench-nailed together and usually without a window, except in villages where there was often a small peep-hole and sometimes also a smaller "Judas door" within the main door. Where you find a steel door, this is a more recent alteration, fitted to provide better security and to overcome the tendency of poorly seasoned timber to warp under the hot, dry conditions.

The few windows were small, rarely more than about 70cm across by 50cm deep (and much smaller than that in the upper floor or loft area), with internal shutters to keep out the summer heat and retain winter warmth. Normally there would be no window in either of the side (gable-end) walls, as these offer no protection from the sun, and are where the chimney stack is most likely to have been located.

The building would have been constructed almost exclusively from local materials at little or no cost, other than the labour of the farmer himself or a local builder who may well have been paid by barter. The beams would have come from a nearby eucalyptus tree, and the bamboo from a clump by the stream at the bottom of the valley. The stone came from the mountain itself, and the clay would also be dug locally.

Other items would have been made in the nearest village, the windows and doors by the carpenter, and the hinges (often of a curious pin-and-cone design) and locks by the blacksmith. Even the roof tiles, the earliest examples being reputedly shaped by the potter pressing the clay against his thigh, would have been made nearby.

Lagares

Looking at the survey map for our immediate vicinity, a surprisingly large proportion of the original houses are described as *lagares* or press-houses. The oldest of these were used to press grapes and contribute to the well-known Málaga wine, until the phylloxera disease decimated the grape harvest and caused many farms to grub up their vines and replace them with olive trees.

Most *lagares* hold clues to the work that went on there in days gone by, and these can help to determine their age. If they were places where grapes were pressed, you are likely to find a huge, heavy, squared-off timber beam across the ceiling (or, as in our case, removed and used nearby to support an extension!). This will have a pivot point at one end, and a threaded hole at the other through which passed the upright timber screw to apply pressure to the grapes. After treading by foot, the pulp was sandwiched between circular woven rush mats for pressing, and some of these may still be around. The juice was then channelled into huge storage pots called *tinajas* sunk into the floor. Other features may also give clues to the original layout and use of the building; we have kept as a feature of the sitting room the chute down which the sacks of grapes were tipped into the treading area (the *pisa de la uva*), as well as several heavy posts built into the thickest of the walls, strapped together with steel bands and hand-cleft nails.

Olive-pressing *lagares* (which, as we explained, are likely to be of more recent construction) would have a more compact type of mechanism consisting of three cone-shaped milling wheels—made of stone in the early days, or of cast iron if more recent—together with a vertical geared device for applying the required turning force.

If you are interested in finding out more about these fascinating old buildings and their uses, the museum in the *Montes de Málaga Parque Natural* contains working examples of each type, and even gives demonstrations during its special open day on one Saturday each September. The exact date varies according to the maturing of the vine harvest, and you can find out exactly when by telephoning 952 11 02 55 a week or two beforehand. The Curator—who speaks English—is also a mine of information.

One of the more obvious clues to the history and layout of our 'lagar' or press-house was this delivery chute, which we have left untouched as a feature of our sitting-room.

Fincas don't suit everyone

A finca does not suit everyone, and it is only fair to point out its drawbacks as well as its charms. Access is invariably along a dirt track that can stretch for many kilometres beyond the nearest main road. During the winter this track can become a sea of mud at times, while in high summer each passing car raises a trail of dust that settles on those living downwind of it.

The climate in the mountains is cooler than in the coastal resorts. Our mountain finca at 750 metres is usually about five degrees cooler than on the Costa—a drop of around one degree Celsius for every 150 metres up. This can be very pleasant in summer but less so during a winter gale. And the wind can blow for several days on end, of a strength which can make it difficult to get on with any outside work. (Not that the coast itself doesn't receive its fair share of gales—it used to be called the "windy coast" before the sol was considered a more marketable description!)

Mains services may not be available. Unless running nearby, it can be difficult to connect electricity and water, and in the campo you can never regard these services as totally reliable.

Do not expect any mail to be delivered, although in our area utility bills always seem to find their way to our door via a network of local contacts. In many remote areas you have to collect your mail from the post office in the nearest village, which is why we were so dependent upon the mobile phone with its fax and internet facilities for keeping in touch with the folks back home.

In the campo you do not have the DIY superstores and building material yards you find down in the coastal areas, and in the campo fewer Spaniards speak your language. Even timber yards are rare, although many local joinery workshops will sell you some timber, sometimes at an inflated price.

But if you have a pioneering spirit and enjoy a challenge, there are advantages to living in a farmhouse in the campo that don't exist in noisy cities or crowded resort towns along the Mediterranean coast.

For a start, there's the peace of it, not just a total absence of noise but rather a deep, rich silence—the most satisfying music on earth—that both fills and clears your mind at the same time. You learn to distinguish between the sounds of different herds of goats many kilometres away on a distant mountain top. And the air is almost intoxicatingly fresh, bearing only the occasional delicious scent of wild herbs.

In fact, living in a mountain top finca is the nearest thing to heaven. Most days you awake to a clear blue sky and the sound of birds. The view outside is so stunning that you never tire of gazing at it.

Before long, the locals pass your finca as they make their way along the track: the old man leading several pack mules, the farmer's truck collecting churns of goat's milk for processing into cheese, the farm workers travelling on foot or on their motorbikes, the tinkling herd of goats followed by the goatherd and a couple of dogs. All of them greet you with a wave and a cheery ¡hola! as they pass.

As the day progresses, the temperature becomes pleasantly warm but without the oppressive heat of the coast, and you begin to relax, aided no doubt by an afternoon glass or two of excellent local wine. You reach for a book but instead you find yourself watching the geckoes as they run along the wall or bask in the sun. A hoopoe flies down a few feet in front of you, becomes aware of your presence and opens its amazing crown of feathers in surprise.

Before you know it, the cool stillness of the evening approaches and, to the faint sound of the goat bells on a distant mountainside, you light up the barbecue. Could the tender *filetes de tenera* and excellent *vino tinto* really have cost so little?

The delicious meal is enjoyed while watching the sun disappear behind the mountains and a gently warm, almost tropical dusk descends. This soon merges into nightfall and you wonder at the amazing number of stars you can see in the clear sky, pausing to watch the slim trail of a shooting star before retiring indoors to relax beside a blazing open fire of gnarled olive logs, to the romantic light of candles or an oil-lamp.

The Andalusian 'campo' at its very best, filled with colourful wild flowers, birds and butterflies. But it's also important to view it at other times of the year before making any major decisions.

Village houses

If you feel reluctant to face the relative isolation of an old farm-house in the campo, you may be better off with a village house, maybe on the edge of the village. In such a location the view can be just as stunning as in the campo itself and you will also benefit from the advantages of easy access, more reliable utility services and closer neighbours. Such a property would also cost less than a house in the campo, which may leave you with money in hand to renovate or improve it. However, it's only fair to warn you that villages can be quite noisy places, with unsilenced mopeds roaring up and down the streets well into the night and loud music emanating from the local bars.

Two general views of the agricultural village of Colmenar—sometimes described as the capital of the Málaga Mountains. It sits in this fold in the hills, with the more fertile land with crops of olives, almonds and vines in the foreground and the rugged Sierra mountains behind to the north and east. It has a population of 3,200; altitude 694 metres; average slope 28%; annual rainfall 744.5mm (29.3 in.); annual sunshine 2800 hours (7.7 hours per day), average temperature 12.6 °C. Crops: almonds, olives, wheat, barley, beans, oatmeal, chickpeas, grapes.

The village is important

When deciding in which area to search for your finca, take a look at nearby villages. You are likely to be visiting your nearest village several times a week for necessary provisions, and it helps if you find this an enjoyable experience.

Spanish villages are very different to their counterparts in many other countries. The comparison between Colmenar—a typical Spanish mountain farming village—and our village in Hampshire is particularly interesting and relevant, as each is a medium to large sized village, and is much the same distance from the south coast. Both have butchers, dentists, hardware shops and a regular bus service into the nearest town, but there the similarities end. One big difference is that Colmenar has proportionately far fewer houses, often occupied by a larger extended family spanning two, three or even four generations. Back home we can no longer enjoy the services of a single bank in the village, yet Colmenar has two to serve less than half as many inhabitants. We have a couple of general food stores at home, rather than fifteen or so in Colmenar. We can't offer the facilities of a library, police station, health centre with ambulance, builder's merchant or weekly street market, yet Colmenar has all of these. What we do have in abundance are yellow lines and public car parks, all of which Colmenar seems to manage without. And our farmers don't lead their mules through the living room to their stables each night. For that matter, we don't even have many farmers left. And not a single mule, to the best of our knowledge.

The facilities in many other villages also compare favourably with their counterparts in other countries. The prevalence of mules doesn't indicate a backward country, for nothing else is quite as efficient at carrying heavy sacks of harvested olives or almonds up the side of a precipitous slope, or transporting farmers and their heavy loads along mountain paths that are too narrow or steep for anything else.

Two pictures taken outside our finca: typical passing 'traffic' is likely to include plenty of mules and goats.

CHAPTER 2

FINDING YOUR FINCA

Mountain or valley? Finding an agent. Choosing your finca. Local services you may need. Exploring the surroundings.

Unless you already know Spain quite well as a result of spending holidays in different areas over several years, you have a lot of research ahead of you. The first step can be spent in the comfort of your home on the internet, or in the local library, comparing the virtues of different parts of Spain, tracking down property agents, asking for particulars. These may serve to encourage you, but nothing can replace the legwork that follows—and this can entail several visits if you want to find your ideal corner in a large and unknown land.

There are so many attractive areas throughout southern and eastern Spain—and, indeed, in other regions less well known to foreigners—that we hesitate to pick out any for special mention. Almost anywhere up in the mountains, and not too far from the coast, could be worth a closer look.

There are, however, a few undesirable features to avoid. In particular, parts of the fertile valley between the coast and mountains are covered by vast areas of plastic greenhouses and mulch sheeting in the quest to produce more and more food in a hot, dry environment, and this is really unsightly. You won't want to look out on acres of that when you wake up each morning, so I'd suggest you give those parts a miss.

Elsewhere the choice is up to you. You may prefer the convenience and relative bustle of being on the outskirts of a Spanish village—or, at the opposite extreme, you may prefer to be hidden away at the end of a perilous track that discourages all but the most determined of visitors. You may be prepared to pay a premium in order to live fairly near to the coast, knowing that your property is likely to retain that extra value. You may prefer to be within easy reach of an airport so that you can easily visit at a moment's notice, or because the property will then be easier to let —but be warned that the occasional airport taxi may refuse to take you along a dirt track beyond the nearest pueblo.

With so many factors to consider, you should allow plenty of time for finding the ideal place—and make up your mind to enjoy the search. If you really can't spare that much time, you can engage an independent location agent to do much of the legwork for you, and send you reports and recommendations.

Mountain or valley?

Mountain-top locations are not for everyone, and their spectacular views and unpolluted air can be offset by drawbacks that can include limited shelter from the frequent strong winds, the risk of an occasional lightning strike, an abundance of pylons, and less reliable water pressure.

As a result, many choose to live in the shelter of the lower slopes or even the valley bottom. This can also reduce the cost of the property considerably, yet the view up a mountain can be almost as impressive as that looking down from the top.

What's more, the extra fertility can result in welcome green shade on a baking hot summer's day, the opportunity to grow tropical plants and fruit, and a degree of shelter from the winter gales. There is, however, one possible snag to watch out for. Drainage systems in Spain are still in the process of improvement in some rural areas, and a few of the oldest systems still disappear into unmapped regions of the campo, downhill from the village. This situation is improving, but meanwhile you should let your nose be your guide.

Another factor that can affect price is the access, particularly if along a long, difficult track. This can result in a bargain provided you're willing to exchange the family hatchback for a 4WD vehicle (but do be sure to investigate the condition of that track during the winter storms in case it becomes loose and unstable to a point beyond the abilities of even such a vehicle).

This crudely made seat occupies our favourite viewpoint, from where we can see both the snow-capped mountains to the north and the warmer Mediterranean sea. Wherever you go in the Spanish countryside, stunning views are almost guaranteed.

A few thousand square metres of land will probably be included in the sale. This could amount to less than an acre (4046 square metres), but it still has to be tended and kept free of weeds. It will also be your moral responsibility to prevent it becoming overgrown to the point where it can present a fire hazard in late summer.

It is often possible to find a neighbouring farmer (maybe even the original vendor) who will be willing to look after the land in return for harvesting the olives or other crops, but you may not welcome this intrusion or you might want to keep the produce for yourself.

Bear all these factors in mind when assessing the area. Viewed objectively, an area of rocky, fairly bare and relatively infertile mountainside can be a more sensible proposition than lush fertile pastures which will be very efficient at growing weeds while you are absent.

Avoid being over-ambitious in your aims for the land. It is easy to get excited at the thought of planting some oranges, lemons, figs or grapes for your own use, but you must remember that newly planted trees need constant watering before they are properly established.

Even then, the only crops that can really flourish without irrigation are olives, prickly pears and usually almonds (see Chapter 14 on looking after your land).

Finding an agent

When in any unfamiliar country, it's sensible to adopt a slightly more cautious approach to choosing a property agent or agencia *inmobiliaria* than you would in your home country. Most of those I've come across seem to be sound, honest and reasonably efficient, but use your common sense before placing your faith (and your cash) in their hands.

Assess their business efficiency in the same way that you would in your home country. Do they always answer the telephone promptly? Do they have a regular office, but also give you a mobile number for urgent, out-of-hours enquiries? (Remember you will need to contact them countless times if you buy a property through them.) Are they always pleasant and courteous when you make an enquiry? Do they seem efficient, send out details promptly and keep their website up-to-date? Do they return your call if you leave a message or send a fax? Are they registered with a recognised trade association? (Look for the certificate on display in their office, and the registration number on their signboard.)

Choosing your finca

When we were viewing a seemingly endless string of properties, we made a check list (described in greater detail later on) and we ran off some copies on our computer printer which we took with us and completed on the spot. We also photographed the more suitable properties.

Our priorities were a stunning view, good access along a sound track that wasn't too long, a really quiet location, a building with bags of character and at least one dry and secure room which was good enough to camp in during the building work. Your priorities may be quite different. Yours could include access to public transport, the company of other ex-pats living in the area, lots of land, close to the sea, a level plot and so on.

One essential item of equipment we took on our inspection trips was a compass, especially helpful during the cloudier days of winter. We not only wanted a place that faced south or south-west but, more importantly, an unobstructed view to the west or northwest, so that we could gain the maximum enjoyment from a balmy summer evening right through to the sunset.

We also realised that south-facing windows let in little heat when the sun is virtually overhead during the height of the summer, which is a good thing, whereas south-west or west-facing windows can make a room unpleasantly warm at a time when you would prefer it to be cooling down for the night. Look for shade, too, whether in the form of a large spreading eucalyptus tree, as in our case, or a bamboo-covered pergola.

An unpromising first view of Corazones on St Valentine's day. With no water or drainage, a burned-out electricity cable, sagging roofs, one leaning wall and a damp interior, it obviously needed some serious help.

When viewing, the agent usually offers to take you around various properties. or you can choose to go in your own car and inspect a property on your own. While it's nice to have the full conducted tour, you can assess the condition of the track much better if you drive yourself, and it's easier to stop looking when you feel tired. However, we wouldn't advise going it alone if you have a long list of properties to see. Some of them could be difficult to find and may be locked up when you do find them.

When you do get inside a building, don't be too discouraged if you see a number of geckoes scurrying across the walls and ceiling. They will lead a more secretive life after you move in, but they will still help to keep the spider and fly population in check; these shy, lizard-like creatures with suckers on their feet are favourites of ours and are definitely to be encouraged.

Check the headroom inside the house, as it seems that past generations of Andalusian farm workers were often quite short in stature. The older the finca, the lower its doorways and ceilings are likely to be!

We suggest that you make a note of any furniture you find within the finca, as this could be offered to you as part of the sale and yet disappear before you take possession. It's worth taking a few inside photographs at this stage, to remind you what the place looks like when decision time arrives. A digital camera is useful as you can review the results of your day's search in greater detail on a laptop computer immediately you return to your hotel or other temporary accommodation.

Our basic requirements included one room that was habitable. This was it— when turned into a temporary bedroom, it reminded everyone of a prison cell.

Explore the surroundings

When you find a place that interests you, make a return visit on your own. Take plenty of time to explore the surrounding area in all directions. Are the nearby walks interesting or will you need to use the car each time you want to go for a day out in the countryside?

Sit down by the house and relax, taking in the atmosphere. Is this really somewhere you would feel at home and want to spend a substantial part of your future life? How friendly do the neighbours or passers-by seem to be? Is the track reasonably sound and the access not too steep? Is the land in good shape? Are there some interesting walks around?

If the place seems perfect but the view is obstructed by a prominently placed pylon on your own land, it is quite possible that this can be moved or your cable put underground—at a price. So don't necessarily exclude such a place from further consideration. Similarly, access drives can be levelled or widened, low doorways can often be increased in height, top-soil can be imported. Be prepared to overlook any shortcomings which can be changed, and only worry about those which obviously cannot.

If you are really serious, stay there as long as you can—preferably until dusk. Is it still just as peaceful or do the local dogs join together in a combined howl? Is there anything else that might possibly prove a future annoyance to you?

Your decision may also depend upon the proximity of various facilities that you might need. It is easier to compare properties if you prepare a list of questions and run off a few copies. We had our own list (which I've included in the website, www.fincabook.com), but your needs may be quite different to ours, so we'll just suggest a few things that you might want to include.

We have already mentioned accessibility, a good view to the south and west, how quiet the area is and obviously the condition of the property and the services and utilities supplied. On top of those you might like to add the following questions.

If you are settling for good, a school would be one of the main priorities if you have a young family, so where is it and what is it like? Is there a school bus? What about medical and dental facilities? Is there an English-speaking doctor in the village? How easy is it to reach the village in an emergency during adverse weather conditions? Where is the nearest hospital? Does it have an Accident and Emergency ward? Is there an interpreter or receptionist who speaks good English?

What about shops? You might be prepared to travel some distance for a major weekly or fortnightly shopping trip, but you will still need to "top up" with fresh bread, meat and fruit at a local store. (Milk is less of a problem as the special long-life milk sold in Spain is surprisingly good).

If you do not intend to buy or hire a car, are you close enough to the village to have gas bottles delivered? What is the public transport situation? Are communications good? If the option of a landline telephone is not open to you, can you receive a strong mobile (cell phone) signal from inside or immediately outside the finca?

Is there a public swimming pool in the vicinity if you don't intend to install your own? Is there an internet café anywhere near? Does the postman deliver to the area or will you have to collect your mail from the nearest town or village?

Anything that passes all those criteria is worthy of serious consideration, and you may wish to place an offer. Before doing so, we suggest that you carefully study a comprehensive book on the legal aspects of buying property in Spain. "You and the Law in Spain" published by Santana Books is the one most foreigners buy.

You should also take advice from a surveyor or, at very least, ask a local builder to take a look at the place and advise you on the cost of any structural work he considers necessary. You will find more advice on this aspect in the next chapter.

CHAPTER 3

TAKING STOCK

Assessing the condition of an old finca, and the cost of rectifying major structural problems. Making an offer. Restoration terms explained. Defining your objectives. Drawing up plans. Grants. Major alterations. Researching a building's history.

Assessing a ruin

Only a professional surveyor can give you an accurate assessment of the condition of a ruined finca, and the work likely to be involved in its repair. Alternatively, obtain advice from a local builder. The property agent can usually recommend one or the other, and the agent will then be aware of the cost of the necessary repairs if you make a reduced offer on that basis.

However, there are a few things you should look out for, which will give you some indication as to whether it is economically repairable.

Our finca at its very worst—the moment when everyone wonders what on earth they've taken on. We often look back at this picture (taken by our friend John Sutherland-Hawes) whenever we need reassurance of our subsequent progress.

First take a very general look at the appearance of the roof from the outside. Are the tiles in good condition or are they starting to crumble and chip? Most importantly, position yourself so that you can look directly up the slope of the roof. Any dip will then be apparent, and this is the first sign of a less-than-perfect roof.

It could mean the beams were never big enough to support the weight or the roof may be leaking, making the clay content much heavier, or the beams may be partially rotten or worm-infested, reducing their strength. Whatever the reason, the problem can only get worse with time, and you should keep a reserve in your budget to get the roof replaced at the earliest opportunity.

The reason for the sagging roof may be more apparent when viewed from within. Check for any damp patches or, if the weather has been dry for some weeks, signs of staining. Push a penknife firmly into the end of some of the beams, just where they enter the wall. It should be almost impossible to push it into eucalyptus, difficult to push into chestnut but a little easier into pine. If it goes in with little resistance, the wood is starting to rot at its most critical and vulnerable point. You'll find more on roof construction and repair in Chapter 8.

What about the walls? Ignore any small areas of "spalling" where the outer coat of lime has erupted outwards, as these loose patches are easily rectified, but large reddish areas are more serious and indicate that the clay is softening or washing out, thus affecting the strength of the wall.

Look closely at the overall shape of the walls. Are they upright? Do they bow when viewed along their length? Don't expect an ancient building to be perfect, but any serious distortion may need repair. Inspect the corners in particular; if any of these have large cracks, or if you suspect that previous cracks have been filled for the purposes of sale, try and discover the reason.

Usually the top of the failing wall will have been unprotected from exposure to rain due to roof damage, causing the clay to soften. To determine how serious this may have become would need the services of a surveyor. Sometimes all that is needed is filling the corner, repairing the roof and drying out the offending wall, but it could be that a ring beam needs to be fitted around the complete property to tie it all in together, or the damaged wall may have to be rebuilt.

Making an offer

Neither of these two repair options is so expensive that it need discourage you from making an offer, although the price should reflect the condition. If not, your bid should be reduced to allow for the extra costs and upheaval. So, when the true condition of the property is known—whether from professional advice or as a result of your own research—you should re-read the fact sheet on the property, take a look at the price and compare it with others in the area, deduct the cost of any necessary building repairs, and prepare to face the seller's agent.

Stressing your seriousness to buy and the fact (if applicable) that it will be a cash offer with no property to be sold or loan to be negotiated before you can complete the purchase, offer him maybe 95% of the adjusted figure you have reached. It may not be accepted outright but at least it will set negotiations rolling.

If your offer is accepted, or a fair compromise price agreed, all documents you are likely to be shown—particularly the *escritura* or transfer deed, and the purchase contract—will be written in Spanish, and it is important to know exactly what they say. Even if you have a fair grasp of the language, you could still be baffled by some of the legal terms used. Your agent or lawyer might offer you a translation service. If not, they could most likely put you in touch with the nearest official translator.

Restoration definitions

To a purist involved in architectural heritage, the word "restoration" means using only original materials and techniques to restore the building to its original condition in all respects. If you decide to go along the purist path, you may be surprised to hear that you're not alone, and if you have access to the internet you'll be able to study many sites devoted to the restoration of historic buildings.

Most of us, however, simply want the house we live in to be dry, warm, light and comfortable. This may mean that certain compromises have to be made if the building concerned is to be used as a residence rather than a historic monument. This was certainly the case with *Corazones*. We have therefore been involved in a process which differs from pure restoration in that additional or different materials to those in the original fabric are used when necessary. This is described by the purists as "adaptation"; we think of it as common sense.

Nevertheless, it is important to respect the views of the preservationists—if only for the reason that there must have been a certain amount of sound thinking behind the construction of a building that has withstood the elements for two or three hundred years—and keep those changes to a minimum so that as much as possible of its original character is retained. After all, the building which you intend to buy is part of the heritage of Spain, and cannot be replaced once it is destroyed.

As in most countries, you will probably find that you are allowed to *repair* an original feature which may not entirely conform to current building regulations, but if you *replace* it completely you may need to bring it in line with modern standards. Bear this in mind when planning your reform work, and—if in doubt—always check with the Ayuntamiento.

Defining objectives

Before you start preparing plans, it is helpful if you can define your objectives:

* Do you want to live there permanently or keep it as a holiday home?

* If it is intended as your holiday home, at what time(s) of year will you be living there?

* Will you need to accommodate houseguests for any length of time, and if so what is the maximum likely number at any time?

DECIDE WHICH YOU REALLY NEED!

Holiday Home	Permanent Home
Possibly less expensive—financed out of your savings or current earnings	After selling your main home you can probably afford to spend rather more
More basic furnishings in case you rent to others	Furnished for all-year-round comfort
Higher level of security may be needed if frequently unoccupied	Normal level of security but bearing in mind local conditions and value of contents
Should be easily cleaned and maintained	More time may be available for looking after your home
Of minimum size necessary to accommodate your family and any expected guests	Large enough for family, guests, and all your possessions and hobbies
Any land should need minimum attention	Can have large, attractive/productive garden needing regular watering
Easily accessible from airport	May be further from airport
Landline telephone less important	Landline telephone more important

* Do you want to generate an income from letting the property when you're not there yourself? If so, it may be worthwhile incorporating facilities like a swimming pool, which you may not need yourself, in order to attract clients.

* Do you want it to be luxurious, comfortable or basic?

* Will you be working from the finca and consequently need an office or a workshop?

* Is your main aim to restore it to its historically correct state or do you intend to convert it to modern living?

* Do you want the surroundings to be natural, productive, ornamental or luxurious (e.g. with a swimming pool)?

Your answers to these questions will play a major role in determining the layout and contents of the house and land. Be prepared to reconsider even the most basic aspects. For instance, is it possible to exist without mains water or electricity? Properties are available at bargain prices in cases where there is little likelihood of being able to connect to these main services at an affordable cost. What's it really like to live without facilities which most people regard as necessities?

If you're looking for a get-away-from-it-all type of holiday cottage, this Spartan approach might be worth considering. However, most people decide that water, drainage and electricity are indeed essential services, and this book explains exactly what is involved in getting these connected and fully operational. And, while waiting for this to happen (which, in Spain, may take longer than you imagine), make up your mind to enjoy the simple life.

Believe it or not, it's really quite easy to make the transition from plush centrally-heated home life to cooking over the embers of an open fire, and it's also fun. There's a trace of pioneering spirit in most of us, given the chance to make itself evident. This is especially the case when there's no hurry to do anything in particular and so you can enjoy the task in hand.

Even washing up becomes a pleasure when it's done alfresco in the warm sunshine against a backdrop of spectacular mountain scenery. Our outside shower—the only one we had for the first eighteen months—became more acceptable (even throughout most of the winter months) because of two things—its ample supply of hot water, and its distant sea view!

Of course this basic life-style can lose its novelty value after a while, but why not enjoy it while you are turning your ruin into a comfortable home? Roughing it for a few months will make you appreciate the comforts even more later on.

Preparing Plans

While all the paperwork to buy your finca is being processed, you can make good use of the time by drawing up your plans. To do this, you need to take detailed measurements on site, and some inside and outside photographs can also help.

If you plan to make major changes or extensions you'll need a long measuring tape: preferably 10 metres long, or a surveyor's tape is even better if you can borrow one. First take the measurements and write them down on a rough overall sketch of the building. Always take running measurements—all from the same point, rather than lots of individual numbers which you must add together—as that method is more accurate. And don't mix metres, centimetres and millimetres. Stick to just one of these, preferably millimetres. For example, if there's a section of wall that's 5.6 metres long, then a door that is 90cm wide, another metre of wall and then a window is 55.5cm wide, your measurements should be 5600, 6500, 7500 and 8055 respectively, because you're counting in millimetres and adding them up as you go.

Walls occasionally lean or are slightly thicker at the bottom for stability, so you'll get in a frightful muddle unless you take all measurements at a given height. One metre off the ground is the usual standard, but you can use windowsill height if it's more convenient. Start by measuring one wall externally and then compare it to the opposite wall. Is it exactly the same? If not, try to discover the reason for this. Almost certainly in an old finca, one or more of the corners will not be square. You then need to go inside if you want to take the measurements necessary for your plan to show the exact angle.

It's not a bad idea to knock together a large set-square out of timber battens measuring 3, 4 and 5 units along each side as the job becomes easier once you have discovered at least one corner that is truly square, from which point you will start to draw your final plan.

If the floor is tiled, the tiles will also give a good indication of which corners are square. In any event, take diagonal measurements across the inside as well, as these can be transferred to the plan and will help to get the overall shape correct. For these diagonal measurements to be of any real help you will also need to check the thickness of the walls, so measure these at convenient points such as at door and window openings.

Now add to your plans the positions of existing drains, water supply pipes, power sockets, lights and so on, as it's best to arrange any future fitments around these if possible. Also measure door and window sizes and heights. It's important to know if the kitchen window is at least 1.1m above the floor to allow the sink and floor units to be fitted comfortably below them. Remember to indicate on your sketch the side on which doors and windows are hinged, and the direction in which they open.

Now you can draw the finished plans, for which you will need the following as a minimum: a few sheets of plain white paper in A3 and A4 size, well sharpened pencils, a plastic eraser and a scale rule. The scale rule doesn't need to be one of the more expensive triangular-shaped devices with six different scales; all you really need are 1:50 and 1:20. If you need to cover a larger area at 1:100, such as general or location plans for planning permission, you can work these out with a normal metric rule by drawing metres as centimetres, and tens of centimetres as millimetres. But generally you'll find that you can draw your entire finca at a scale of 1:50, while even the largest room can be drawn at 1:20 on A4 paper.

Grants

Don't get carried away by the idea that you may be able to offset your costs by obtaining a substantial subsidy or grant, although it's something you should certainly investigate at an early stage. First you have to track down your grant. Any that are available tend to vary from one region to another, according to local needs and policy. In some areas you may be able to get a grant for replanting or improving your land. Most villages have their own grower's co-operative, and facilities may include olive pressing, almond de-husking, the sale of fertilisers, and technical advice when needed.

Most grants seem to originate from the EU and are intended to cover specific needs such as rural tourism, energy efficiency, preservation of the architectural heritage and redevelopment of depressed areas. Some are offered directly from the EU but the great majority of these tend to go to organisations rather than individuals and are for specific projects of a more altruistic nature, such as restoring an ancient monument of particular public interest. Information on such specialised grants is published by a service known as CORDIS (Community Research and Development Information Service) which is located in Luxembourg.

This has its own website on www.cordis.lu and there are links to related sites. All grants and aids that come from the EU are listed at: http://europa.eu.int/comm/secretariat_general/sgc/aides/index_e n.htm. However, it is only fair to warn you that it can be extremely time consuming to find what you need among these massive and often confusing sources of official information.

Applications for any type of grant inevitably involves filling in loads of forms in duplicate and triplicate, submitting detailed plans, obtaining multiple quotations from professional builders and generally convincing the fund source that you are a worthy cause to support. Delays are frequent. Generally you need to have all the work carried out by a professional builder, and even then the grant will only cover part of the cost. Often conditions are imposed which are inconvenient or even detrimental to the value. Getting help towards restoring a prominent and historic building to its original state could oblige you to open it to the public.

You might well decide, as we did, that it is quicker and cheaper to undertake much of the work yourself. However, it makes good sense to find out all you can about possible grants and subsidies so that you can make your own reasoned decision about whether to apply. However, if you do manage to reduce your improvement costs by whatever method, and you eventually decide to sell the finca, you should bear in mind that you will end up paying tax on a larger capital gain. In the light of that, employing a builder may become a more attractive proposition!

Major alterations

Having produced your outline plan, think carefully how to make the best use of the space. Decide first what are your minimum essential requirements, and make a list. If you need two or more bedrooms start your list with that. You will obviously need a kitchen, dining room and quite possibly a separate living-room, but can two or more of these be combined? Do you need an en-suite toilet and shower, if only to provide your guests with their own facilities? And how about a study, a workshop, a storage room, or improved access to a loft area?

Now cut up some pieces of card, representing your main items of furniture and fittings to the same scale as the plan. You'll need a dining table and chairs, beds, bedside units, wardrobes, at least a couple of metres of kitchen worktop with fridge and oven beneath, a sofa and so on.

Start to juggle those around and you'll soon see whether your space is adequate for your needs. If it is, then all you must do is decide a practical layout for the rooms, sub-dividing what you already have if necessary. If you cannot fit everything you need into the available space, then decide just how much of an exten-sion is likely to be needed and incorporate this into your plans from the outset.

Before making too many irreversible steps involving plumb-ing and major rewiring, we recommend you put your new arrangements to a practical test for a month or two, even if this means a degree of inconvenience from temporary expediencies like trailing extension leads or a bucket under the sink to catch the waste.

You will soon find out what, if any, further changes are need-ed. You might want to enlarge the window above the sink or put in a new doorway to provide direct access to the outside. Alterations like these involve a major degree of mess, and it is essential to get such work out of the way before installing fit-ments that are easily damaged.

Researching a property's history

Having found your old finca, you may be interested to discover something of its history. Unfortunately, because of the way a new escritura is prepared each time the property is sold, it can be quite difficult to research the history of a Spanish finca.

The first step is to mention your interest in the history of the building to the Notary when making the arrangements for the legal transfer. Although he is likely to be a very busy person, he will probably be pleased that you are taking an interest in the history of the area and his local knowledge can be invaluable. He keeps the original documents of each transaction and the new owner receives only a certified copy.

If you have already bought the property or are making enquiries before doing so, you could visit the Town Hall (the *Ayuntamiento*), taking with you copies of all documents relating to the sale, so that the property can be easily identified. They will already have supplied copies of all locality maps and plans they have on file in response to pre-purchase enquiries through your agent, and they are unlikely to have anything else relating to the property unless it is of particular historic interest and significance. Nevertheless, it's worth asking, particularly as the Town Hall may have one or two English-speaking officials in case your grasp of the Spanish language is limited.

If your enquiries at the Town Hall draw a blank, you should try the regional land registry, as all transfers of ownership of land and property have to be registered there. The Town Hall will be able to tell you where this is—usually in the capital town of your province.

Although Spain is as interested in its heritage as most other countries, its museums and researchers tend to be mainly involved with the arts and city architecture. Few seem to show much interest in mere farm buildings and rural workplaces. One notable exception is the rural museum in the *Montes de Málaga Parque Natural*, described in the first chapter. Also, the regional council of Andalucía has produced a beautifully illustrated coffee-table type book devoted to old properties in the area which is a joy to own, even though it includes only a limited selection of important buildings in each area.

You can find a complete list of Spanish museums on the internet, with contact details for each in case you have any queries relating to their specialised subjects (see Chapter 18 on the internet).

CHAPTER 4

HOME IS WHERE YOUR TOOLS ARE

Shipping goods out—removals firms, driving down yourself. What to take and what to buy. Behind closed doors -finding materials and services. Tools you may need. Looking after your tools.

Transporting your tools

The moment when our first delivery of furniture and tools arrived. Several international removals firms offer a regular delivery service to Spain, carrying anything from a single box to the contents of a complete home.

If you are not already a resident in Spain when you buy your finca, you'll inevitably have many tools and household goods you will want to take with you. Even if you only intend to use your finca as a holiday home, you will still need tools, and there is no point in buying a complete set of replacements if you already have some which can be spared. So how do you get them to Spain as cheaply as possible?

One method we have always found to be reliable and reasonably priced between the UK and Spain is to send a few tea-chest sized boxes with a removal firm offering a regular delivery service for part loads. You can find advertisements from many of these companies in the various free English newspapers and magazines available in Spain, or via the www.surinenglish.com website. Such companies will even supply the empty boxes, collect and deliver if required. Other options include taking the things with you on the plane, asking friends who are driving to see you to find space for them in their car, or driving down with them yourself by road and/or ferry.

When choosing between transporting by plane and truck, remember that airlines charge excess baggage by weight, whereas removal firms are more concerned with volume. So it pays to send the small, heavy things by van and the big, bulky items, such as your bed quilt, as baggage on the aircraft. Airline check-in staff usually have the authority to negotiate over excess baggage charges and, if you're nice to them, they will usually overlook the odd kilo or two, especially if the aircraft isn't full.

The decision you take about driving down to Spain with your goods depends, we suppose, on how much you enjoy long drives and whether you intend to use your foreign-registered car in Spain, or buy a car in Spain; in the campo, there is no option to manage without one, and long-term hire would be an expensive overhead.

What to take

When deciding what goods to take in the way of either household goods or tools, first make sure they are (a) difficult or impossible to obtain in Spain and (b) absolutely necessary to your restoration. It's so annoying to buy something elsewhere, followed by the additional cost of getting it shipped out, only to find that you could have bought it in Spain for half the price. On the other hand, you might prefer to ship some goods out to save the trouble of tracking them down in Spain at a time when you are likely to be fully occupied with your restoration project.

One thing we decided to take out with me, and which proved to be extremely useful, was a bread-maker, as these aren't so common in Spain. It's wonderful to wake up to the smell of freshly baked bread each morning, and the need for a daily trip to the bakery in the nearest village is eliminated. At first the quality of our home-baked loaves was disappointing, until we found that some of the flour sold to us for bread-making was not the correct "strong" or "hard" type. We now buy our flour directly from the local village bakery, five kilos at a time, scooped straight from the sacks from which they make their own bread.

Behind closed doors

It's not always easy for an outsider to track down the right craftsmen, materials or services you'll need when fitting out your finca. At first, we could spend several days tracking down a single supplier. Over a period of time, we got to know the system better. We learned that behind many a closed village door lurked a specialist supplier or tradesman.

Very often there's not even a sign above the door, and they seem to do nothing to advertise their wares. Spanish craftsmen, on the whole, prefer to rely on word-of-mouth to promote their services. With village bars playing such a vital part in their social life, anyone who does a good job at a fair price receives all the free advertising he needs, and it becomes common knowledge that Paco the Plumber or Julio the Joiner is the man to contact if the need arises. The only way to find the man you need is to ask— either in the bars or in any of the local shops, preferably one in which you are a regular customer.

When dealing with local tradesmen, bear in mind that half of the people in a village seem to be related in one way or another, so it pays to be courteous and discrete, or else you'll soon gain a reputation as an *antipático* or disagreeable foreigner.

There are plenty of trades people who do advertise their services in local English-language newspapers. In the past these have mainly been ex-pats, who have the advantage of being able to speak English but who may not always have the necessary local experience. More recently, Spanish tradesmen are also advertising in these newspapers, so there are signs that yet another change is taking place.

Even after finding a supplier of the specialised goods or services you need, you are then faced with the problem of conveying to them (often in very broken Spanish) what it is you need. More often than not, the words we needed were not even in the dictionary. Pictures were the only answer, so we used to go prepared with cuttings from English catalogues, scribbled sketches on shopping lists. Usually these worked, and—by asking them to write down the Spanish word we were after—we gradually expanded our limited vocabulary.

Most of our problems in tracking down suppliers and materials were, in fact, due to our tenuous grasp of the language, combined with our timidity in attempting to communicate. As soon as we grasped the bull by the horns and started asking the right questions, eventually we always seemed to find someone who had the right answers. The local "Yellow Pages" is also useful, but difficult to obtain if you don't have a phone account; you may be able to persuade a local business to pass on their previous year's copy. When we became really desperate to find out such information, we would sometimes contact one of the English tradesmen advertising in the local English-language newspapers, who were usually kind enough to help.

If you're living way out in the campo and have had little opportunity or need to visit larger towns and cities, you may not realise that there are DIY hypermarkets in Spain. Look out for names such as Texas Hiperhogar, Leroy Merlin and Aki. Even the larger food hypermarkets such as Eroski often have good DIY, gardening and motoring sections, although they tend to steer clear of actual building materials. (To help you find the things you need, you'll find a short list of useful Spanish phrases in Chapter 15.)

Tools you may need

The jobs you decide to tackle in and around your Spanish finca will largely determine what tools you will need. Inevitably, no matter how many useful tools you take with you, the very thing you need for an urgent job was left behind and you'll have to buy another.

Personally, I decided to start by taking out all duplicate tools I have accumulated over the years—and then some more. So I began with the all-important electric drill. I certainly owned several of these, but were they the right type? What I needed in Spain was a powerful drill that would also hammer holes deep into the stone walls, often a long way from the power point. What I possessed was a mains hammer drill, a mains non-hammer drill and a rechargeable non-hammer drill. None was ideal on its own—so, after comparing prices in England and Spain, I decided to send out the hammer drill and the battery drill, and I treated myself to a new rechargeable hammer drill for use at home.

Some tools which were relatively expensive, yet were only needed for a once-off job (like the electric chain-saw I needed for cutting up dozens of old wooden roof beams for use on our wood-stove, and also the tool for cutting wall tiles) I took out and returned afterwards. Admittedly such tools can be hired in Spain, but this is fairly expensive and could be a problem if you live far from the nearest hire depot as they don't normally offer a delivery service.

With many other tools I had a greater level of success. I had a mains electric wood planer and several old but well-made hand planes, so I took the best of the hand models. As I rummaged deeper into the tool chest, more and more duplicates came to light—set squares, sets of drill bits, sharpening stones, hammers, chisels, cold chisels, masonry tools. If no spare existed, I bought a new one in Spain, and I carefully resisted the temptation to send out anything that was worn or substandard.

If you come from the UK, it is important when using electrical tools with square plugs on the Spanish supply to make quite sure (by testing with a continuity meter, if possible) that the adaptor you use correctly connects the earth of the tool to the earth of the mains supply, and press the RCD test button on the distribution board to ensure that this essential protective device works. This is especially important when using such tools outdoors.

I have compiled a complete list of the tools which I have found necessary for our restoration. However, the list is a long one and it won't interest everyone, so I've included it in the website, www.fincabook.com, for those who may find it a useful check.

Looking after your tools

It pays to take good care of your tools. After Alec uses anything, it gets cleaned and oiled. Even the cement mixer gets a wax polish once in a while! Some may consider that's going a bit too far, but we are convinced that it actually saves us time, for it is such a quick job and yet it ensures that no cement ever builds up around the drum.

Paint brushes are cleaned scrupulously after use, particularly after using oil paints. No special brush cleaner is needed—just several dips in white spirit (*simil de aguarras*) or universal solvent (*disolvente universal*), followed each time by a wipe on a soft cloth, then several washes in hot water and washing-up detergent. If we do throw a brush away, it is because the bristles have worn down too far, and never because they're clogged with paint. On the other hand, we know plenty of people who use a fresh brush for each new paint job, which is not too extravagant in Spain as brushes are relatively cheap.

Do not reject Spanish building and garden tools just because some of them look unfamiliar. They are remarkably effective and well suited to local conditions. We explain in Chapter 7 how those large, round paintbrushes work wonders on rough walls. The blunt-nosed gauging trowels are ideal for building with stone. The mattocks are excellent tools for working the barren soil, and we like the way you can get them with the blade at different angles to suit the steepness of the mountainside. Although electrical tools can be slightly more expensive in Spain, hand tools are very reasonably priced (even in small, local hardware shops) and there is little excuse for not having the right tool for the job.

CHAPTER 5

FINDING A BUILDER YOU CAN TRUST

Choosing a builder. Someone local? An estimate—what's that? Obtaining permission: rules and regulations. Living on site versus other options.

Choosing a builder

Throughout our lives, we have been closely associated with people who have employed builders. It's an undeniable fact that the great majority of these people end up being dissatisfied with their service. Some are driven to total despair, vowing never to employ another builder ever again—until the next extension comes along.

Having major structural building work carried out in your home can be one of the most stressful events in your life, reputedly rating just below bereavement, divorce, moving home and burglary. We suppose it's the subconscious feeling that your home is being assaulted by those over whom you have less than full control. No matter how good the builders and how considerately they try to minimise the mess, there's always that wonderful sense of relief when they finally leave and you can regain control of your home. Maybe that's why we try and do as much of the work ourselves as possible.

The frustrating thing is that, for most people, a builder is all too necessary. Heavy labouring becomes more of a strain with advancing years, and skills are needed which most of us do not possess. Even if you intend to do much of the internal and finishing work yourself, as we did, you are very likely to need a builder for the heaviest and most technically demanding parts of the work.

We're not sure we are the best people to advise you on how to choose a builder. We met ours in the most casual way imaginable.

We were in the local hardware shop, buying some initial essentials -a fridge, a room heater, some duplicate keys, a bucket, broom, club hammer and trowel—before moving into an abandoned, draughty, unfurnished finca, and our Spanish was barely up to the job.

"Can I help?" said this welcome voice with a strong West Country accent, and we turned to meet its burly owner and his colleague. After helping us to buy various other goods we needed but couldn't name in Spanish, they turned up on the doorstep the very same afternoon and rigged up an efficient temporary electrical distribution board that enabled us to plug in the fridge and start making ourselves at home.

On our previous visit to the area, we had been introduced to two different Spanish builders and obtained from them a rough idea of the cost of the work we envisaged. When we asked John and Richard to quote, we found that their prices were very close. What's more, they were prepared to give written estimates with various options. They were nice to have around, they showed us another similar job they had completed, explained that they could be contacted easily by e-mail or fax from our home country, and they made a good job of the cesspit which we asked them to make as a test project. In the end it was John, together with his Spanish workers José and Antonio, who carried out most of the heavy work for us, and produced a good solid job for us on the parts that really matter.

The gang's all here— and with a JCB and heavy truck in attendance, work begins in earnest.

While you may not find your own builders quite as easily, the criteria we applied to ours is worth following. Most importantly, make sure you are really confident in them before leaving your precious property entirely in their hands, or you may lose many a sleepless night.

Someone local

Despite having decided on employing British builders (albeit with Spanish labourers), we have to admit that there's much to be said for using local people. Most Spanish builders engaged by friends have been both honest and reasonable. Respected members of the local community, they are usually unwilling to risk their reputation by ripping off an innocent *extranjero*. And it's good to help the local economy and establish contact with local tradesmen.

There's also something to be said for asking your property agent to recommend or engage a builder. It may cost a little more, but at least he will be able to convey your precise instructions to the builder, arrange a proper estimate and check that the work is carried out properly if you're not around at the time.

An estimate—what's that?

However, Spanish builders do seem to suffer from one common characteristic. They are often unwilling to give a written estimate. Don't be too alarmed by this. It often means that they are unable to assess the amount of work that may be needed until the job has been started. For example, it is quite normal for part (or more) of a wall to fall down once the roof is removed, and it is almost impossible to predict this accurately in advance.

You will probably be given a verbal, ball-park figure for the main work. Write this down before you forget it, to avoid confusion later. The builder will, if pressed, probably also come up with a further price for other work that may or may not be needed, such as the cost of rebuilding one wall, which you should also note down carefully. Then (with the help of a friend whose Spanish is better than yours if necessary), type out the estimate yourself, giving the builder one copy and keeping another for yourself. Don't upset the builder by adding harsh or restrictive clauses, or by asking him to sign it. Once he has read, agreed and pocketed it, you can be fairly sure it will be honoured.

While the builder is surveying the property for his estimate (whether verbal or written), ask plenty of questions, for you might not have another chance to do so. Prepare yourself in advance with a list of these, and don't be reluctant to ask about aspects of the work which you intend to carry out yourself. Often the agent who sold you the property can be persuaded to accompany you.

Obtaining permission

As soon as you know what building work is needed, and how much it's likely to cost, visit your Town Hall (*Ayuntamiento*) and speak to someone in the Spanish equivalent of the Building Control Department. Normally your builder or property agent will be in a better position to do this for you. If the repair work is relatively minor and the finished result isn't going to look very different, the job is likely to be classed as *obra menor* and no plans or special permission are needed. Just tell them what's happening, then a certificate/invoice is made out to you for the cost of the licence and you take this to your bank to be paid out of your account.

If the Town Hall finds out about the work before you have a chance to pay them a visit, it won't be long before someone comes along with the bill. This may include a small surcharge for your oversight, and you will need to make quite sure that they have correctly interpreted your intentions.

Rules can be interpreted differently from one area to another, and you should take as much information as possible with you to the Town Hall and seek their advice. Fees seem to vary with the type of work that's being carried out. In our case the form covered four categories of work which were all ticked, including the one for changes to the external appearance, and the cost was 418 euros.

No planning permission was required, nor did plans appear to be required, and we assume this was because no extension was involved.

Living on the job—or in the village?

Keeping in touch with progress with your builder when you're back in your home country can be a cause for concern and a potential source of misunderstanding and even mistrust. Such communications issues are discussed in chapter 18, but you might like to consider here one alternative. If you are in a position to spare the time, why not live in a caravan parked on the land? You'll save the cost of an extra return flight, and effectively have a low-cost holiday while making sure the job is done thoroughly. Some people even buy a small village house, for probably no more than a third of the cost of the finca, live there during the building work and then sell it later (probably at a slight overall profit). Or maybe you can rent a flat in the local village. This can be surprisingly inexpensive if you deal direct with the owner, rather than via an agency. Or, if business commitments prevent this, how about asking your partner to do the house sitting? There will be many occasions when you will be glad you had the opportunity of keeping an eye on things and rectifying small mistakes before they become a major problem.

CHAPTER 6

THE STRENGTH LIES IN THE WALLS

What, no foundations? Wall finishes. Wall deterioration. Assessing dangerous walls. Consolidation and repairing walls. Extending walls. Spanish bricks. Rendering and maintenance. External walls. Mortar mixes to use. Making your own lime putty.

As we explained in the introduction, we are aware that few finca owners will want to undertake the major structural work themselves, but it's still very important to know how the walls and roofs are made, and the correct way to repair and extend them, so that you can understand what your builder is doing.

The wall of an old Spanish building is a living thing. Quite unlike the thin, rigid structure of a modern building, it consists of local stone bedded into clay to a thickness of 60 to 80cm or more, dried in the sun and protected by a sound, overhanging roof. Originally these walls were finished in a lime that was water-resistant rather than waterproof, allowing the wall to "breathe" and dry out the naturally rising dampness which is a feature of clay construction.

Traditionalists argue that these old buildings have only endured for hundreds of years because of this well-proved method of construction, and that they should therefore be maintained using the same materials. Others accept that modern building materials can be very useful when maintaining, improving or extending a finca, and we have tried to be fair to both camps in this book.

What, no Foundations?

In mountain areas, the wall will often be built straight on to the bedrock, without any trace of footings. Even in cases of deeper, softer soil the walls won't extend down as far as you might expect and will probably just rest on a layer of binders (stones stretching across the whole width of the wall and set just below the surface). Such buildings were expected to take a generation before they settled completely, after which the structure is in a state of relaxation and comfortable retirement, as opposed to the pre-stressed tension of modern architecture. It's no wonder that people who are in tune with such things find living in a finca to be such a natural and relaxing experience!

What better foundations could you have than the solid rock face of a Spanish mountain?

This may come as a shock to those accustomed to living in rigid brick-built houses, built on solid concrete strip footings and carefully isolated from the damp by an efficient damp proof course. However, a finca's wall has a degree of flexibility that can withstand minor disturbances like daily expansion in the heat of the sun, normal building settlement and even small earth tremors. (Modern homes in the campo tackle this problem by being built on a concrete raft, on which the entire structure can "float".)

In fact, when an ancient finca wall is extended or re-rendered using modern hard, cement-rich impermeable mix (particularly if the new render is thin and poorly attached), it is usually the new material that is the first to crack, and—if neglected—can lead to water entry, softening of the clay mortar, and ultimate collapse. Look for the danger signs: if the render is showing signs of coming loose and sounds hollow when tapped, this is often an indication that water is trapped inside as a result of imprudent renovation work, and further deterioration is likely. In fact, if you look closely at most ruins that are in a really bad state, you will find evidence that they have been inexpertly patched up with cement at some stage prior to their failure.

Despite their lack of any form of damp-proof course, the walls of Spanish fincas are rarely damp. If you come across one which does have a damp problem, as evidenced by soft or flaking plaster or mildewed patches, usually inside, you need to identify the source of the trouble—for there is sure to be one, the source sometimes being some distance away, and usually it can be cured quite easily. The possible causes, and ways of remedying these, are dealt with in a later chapter. But fortunately, many minor damp problems disappear after simply living in the finca for a while, and never return.

Wall finishes

In the oldest fincas, or in parts of more recent buildings that were used as animal housing, the walls will be left with their bare stone finish or covered with a regular brushed-on coat of limewash (whitewash) to disinfect them, to deter the flies and to protect them from the elements. A skilled stonemason would have sloped the stones slightly downwards at the front to enable them to shed rainwater more efficiently, but many fincas were built by the farmer and his family using more basic skills handed down from father to son.

Section of original stone-and-clay wall

The wall in those parts of the finca used for animal housing were still as when originally constructed, and the clay mortar is clearly visible between the stones. Protected by a sound roof, this simple construction has lasted for hundreds of years.

As the appearance of the building became more important, many were coated with lime render and then lime washed to give the smooth, brilliant white finish that was becoming fashionable. Even then, they knew enough to avoid applying a hard coating of cement.

This type of wall construction is by no means restricted to Spain but can be found in almost any part of the world where the essential ingredients of stone and clay are available on the doorstep. If well maintained, it will last virtually for ever.

Deterioration sets in

But even in the relatively dry atmosphere of Spain, deterioration is fairly rapid—usually within decades—once the roof fails. Then water enters the wall, the clay softens, the outer layer washes out (leaving those characteristic red streaks down the wall which are the first warning sign), and the stones start to loosen and fall away. Then the roof beams lose their grip at each end, causing the front and back walls to lean outwards and eventually part company at the corners. At this point the damage becomes irreversible, short of a complete rebuild.

Faced with a building that appears to suffer from more serious structural deterioration, how can you assess its condition and the viability of restoration?

Advice from a builder

The first step is to seek advice from a local builder who is sympathetic to your desire to restore the property, and who has had considerable experience of this type of work. Most, in our experience, will recommend demolishing the old finca—even if the deterioration is minimal—and replacing it with something more modern. This is probably the cheapest option, as it's easy to spend considerably more on a comprehensive restoration project than it would cost to build a new house. With so many fine old buildings being destroyed in this way, it is inevitable that those which remain are increasing in value, which helps to compensate for the extra cost.

Chapter 5 suggests ways of finding a reliable builder. Ideally he should have already restored some fincas and be willing to show them to you. He should know about local conditions, availability of materials and resources, and he'll be able to give you an idea of the cost. And his advice should be free. Just make sure, by viewing some of his previous work, that he takes care to preserve the original character of the building.

Checking for safety

There are certain elementary structural checks that you can carry out for yourself. For instance, suppose a wall looks a bit like the leaning tower of Pisa and you want to decide if it is safe to be tied in to the adjacent wall and left as it is, or whether it is unstable and must be rebuilt. By taking careful measurements and angles, using a spirit level, rule, plumb line and protractor if you have nothing better, draw an accurate cross-section of the wall at its worst point (the angle at which it leans must be very accurately drawn). Now mark on your drawing its centre of gravity. This is easy to calculate if the wall is of even thickness and has a consistent slope, but awkward shapes and sizes will require some knowledge of geometry. Assuming the former to be the case, draw a line connecting top right to bottom left, and top left to bottom right, to find the point at which they cross. Extend this point vertically downwards to see where this falls across the base of the wall.

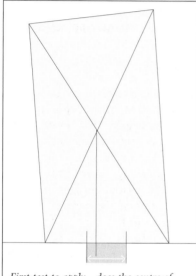

First test to apply—does the centre of gravity lie within the central third of the base?

The general rule is that if this meets the base within the central third of the wall, it can be considered safe, provided it is on sound footings, securely tied in to an adjacent wall and protected from further deterioration by a sound roof. However, this should be considered a useful rule-of-thumb and nothing more, as other factors may be involved which need to be evaluated by a professional. If the lean is anywhere approaching the danger point, or if you consider that it may be increasing rather than stable, you should seek further help.

A cracked wall might be nothing worse than previous settlement that has now stabilised. To check—if you have time to do this test—you can glue slips of glass across the crack and wait as long as possible. If the glass fractures, the wall could have a structural problem.

An external wall needing attention can be rendered under certain conditions. If it is built on solid rock so that no further settlement is likely and is perfectly dry, a cement render (if well bonded into place and of sufficient thickness and strength that it will not crack) can improve both its appearance and its longevity.

But it is still preferable to use a mortar made from real lime, which gives just as much protection and allows the wall to move and breathe just as it has since the day it was built. The technique for making lime putty by slaking lump quicklime, sold as "cal" by most builders' merchants, is described in Chapter 7.

It is very important to know that modern materials will not automatically solve pre-existing problems of stability or dampness, and there is a risk of making these worse in the long run. Such problems should be tackled at source rather than covered up.

Consolidating derelict walls

If part of your finca is really derelict, with a faulty or missing roof and broken walls, and you don't expect to be restoring it in the immediate future, it should be protected against further deterioration. Most importantly, cap the top of the wall to prevent rain penetration, by firmly cementing some old roof tiles on top or casting a temporary concrete slab with a sloping top. This process is one example of what is known as "consolidating as found". An effective temporary protection is an overhanging strip of roofing felt or heavy polythene, held down against the mountain gales by numerous rocks. Rain can easily penetrate the sides of such walls, so it is important to repair any defective render and keep the walls well painted.

Extending walls

Sooner or later you will be faced with the problem of repairing or extending a wall using walling blocks, rendering an existing wall that is deteriorating, or making good after knocking a new opening. How on earth can you persuade this new render to attach itself to the original clay? The answer is, of course, that you can't. Render will only bond to brick, or to stone or existing render if first treated with PVA, and so any clay has to be raked out quite deeply to give a firm key.

To extend a wall upwards, you need to rake out the clay across the top of the joint (to under half a stone's depth, though), clean the stonework, liberally seal exposed areas with PVA according to the instructions, and then lay a good thickness of sharp mortar or fine concrete, tamped down well into the gaps. The same principle applies to surface render, where the existing finish is crumbling away. Cut it well back before refinishing.

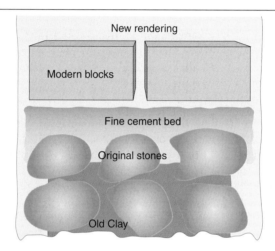

How to solve the difficult problem of building a new wall on an old stone base, a necessary procedure when you cannot find (or afford) a skilled mason.
Bonding the two together is extremely important, using plenty of PVA and even inserting steel reinforcing rods for added strength.

Alternative technique

Another method sometimes used when rebuilding or extending walls is to build up either side to the same overall thickness as the original, using 19x40mm terracotta building slabs, hammer reinforcement rods into the original wall to key the two areas together, and then fill with fine concrete mix.

But why should you want to desecrate your traditionally constructed finca by adding modern materials at all? Ideally you wouldn't. Given all the time in the world and the skill that only comes from generations of skilled masons, you could rebuild or extend your walls using only the original materials and techniques. The fact remains it is far cheaper and quicker to use modern materials. But keep this in mind: if the new area of walling is badly executed or poorly attached, the joint may fail and crack, leading to the entry of water and—if left untreated—the destruction of the old wall at this point. If in doubt, seek local advice before you proceed.

If you decide to go ahead, the skill in combining these materials lies in disguising the modern addition beneath a matching, slightly flexible render that extends the uneven finish of the original stonework. This is quite easy to do, though it's wise to practise first on an unimportant area such as a workshop or garage wall before tackling a prominent part of the finca.

No matter how careful you may be, some cracks are likely to appear within a few months wherever new brickwork or shuttered concrete is built on to existing stone walls. These cracks will be more prevalent if insufficient care had been taken to bond the two very different materials together, using techniques such as treating the masonry with PVA and embedding reinforcing rods into the joint.

You should not be unduly worried by these effects of shrinkage or settlement. Cracks in the outside rendering, which do not extend to the interior, are usually caused by the intense heat of the Spanish sun and are a nuisance but little more. Provided they are not allowing damp to penetrate into the building, we have found it best to leave them until we are sure they are not growing, and then rake them out, treat the surfaces with PVA and fill them with a strong mortar incorporating some PVA in the mixture. You only need be concerned about cracks which extend right through the wall, or which continue to grow, indicating a structural problem.

Repairing outside walls

There are almost bound to be areas of wall that need repairing before they can be rendered. Ideally you would repair them using lime putty (that versatile material made by immersing quicklime in water and maturing for several months). After the repaired section had slowly dried and matured over several weeks, it would then be as flexible and permeable as the rest of the wall. However, the techniques involved are not easily learned, and most people are faced with using modern materials at times.

Where there are quite deep holes and fissures in the wall, it can be tricky to fill these with stones, which provide hardly any suction to the mortar and may be too smooth and round to stay in place. Use instead fragments of broken roof tile, which can be built up several layers high at a time without falling out. It's well worth spending a little time beforehand building up a reserve stock of these pieces from the many you'll find lying around. For larger holes, use pieces of brick.

If nothing else, the bottom of many of your walls are sure to need attention, for this is where the pointing is washed out by the rain from the roof, leaving the stonework vulnerable to further attack by the elements. Often this is eroded to the point where the wall above is structurally weakened, so the damage should be repaired as a matter of urgency.

The bottom of a wall is often severely eroded by rain falling from the roof, which can cause structural damage and work its way indoors (left). The joints should be raked out quite deeply and primed with PVA to ensure that the new mortar provides a permanent and reliable repair (right).

Chop out the cracks quite deeply, paying particular attention to the very bottom layer of stones. Check that these continue right down to the bedrock, or to some substantial footing stones. If this is not the case, and any gaps cannot be readily filled, find out from a builder if underpinning is necessary, particularly if any serious cracks are starting to appear in the wall above. If there are only minor gaps, fill these very thoroughly indeed, building up with pieces of roof tile set in mortar when necessary. Finally render over the entire base with a good coating of mortar to prevent any recurrence of the erosion.

Wall rendering technique

In case you're worried by the thought of rendering a section of wall, let us reassure you—it's easy, and if you're anything like us you'll agree that it's fun. By doing the job yourself, you may take longer than a professional, and you may end up making a bit more of a mess (of yourself, for one thing), but we can assure you that the final result will be every bit as acceptable as it really doesn't need to be perfect.

As with all building and redecorating jobs, the first step is to prepare the surface as thoroughly as possible. This always takes longer than you imagine, but it is time well spent. Hack away all loose matter and surface clay with a bricklayer's hammer and brush well with a stiff brush. Prepare some PVA primer by diluting 1:3 with water, and apply generously into the joints. Now prepare your render, having taken all the factors we have described into account when deciding whether to use a lime putty mixture, or a cement/lime/sand mix. This should be wet but never sloppy, and well aerated by incorporating a special additive, or washing-up detergent, in the mixing water. The acid test is to throw a trowel full against the wall and check whether it sticks. It should spread out slightly but never splatter. If it drops off, it is likely to be too dry.

This throwing technique is something you'll soon pick up, although it may at first sound rather alarming. It's a good way to ensure that the render gets propelled right into the cracks and joints. The alternative technique is to load the render on to a spot board or hawk, or on to the back of a steel float, and then scoop this straight on to the wall with your trowel. If you place a board on the ground along the base of the wall, you'll be able to pick up and re-use render that falls off. The method we prefer is to start at the bottom and work up, as it's easier to smooth upwards without losing too much. As each patch of render is applied, extend the trowel upwards to spread it more evenly.

For smoothing the render on the wall, we prefer to use a round-nosed or gauging trowel, which avoids leaving too many sharp lines; a conventional steel float gives too perfect a finish for such rural properties. Follow the variations of the stonework rather than trying to obtain a perfectly flat finish. In fact, the surface can be left quite uneven, as the final sponging makes all the difference. Ignore trowel marks and just aim at a fairly even coating on each stone at this stage.

If you find the render frequently sags, leaving a gap along the tops of any deeper holes, that is an indication that the wall is too uneven to be rendered in a single coat. Don't worry—just concentrate on the deeper holes alone for the moment, filling these only and leaving a scored finish so that the next coat will key on to it.

Having allowed anything from an hour to six hours depending on temperature, wind, dryness of the underlying wall and the strength of the mixture, the mortar will start to stiffen and start to "go off" as the builder would say. It can now be sponged down quite lightly with an almost saturated decorator's heavy duty sponge, to remove the sharp lines from the trowel and match the surrounding surface finish (or you may find a wide wallpaper pasting brush more convenient). If you try doing this too soon you will find it difficult to smooth the surface without digging into the render, but if you're too late you won't be able to smooth it at all.

The process may sound difficult but it really isn't, and you'll be surprised how easily you can achieve a really professional looking finish.

Some owners go further and add a wedge of concrete along the entire base of the wall, so that water is channelled away from it.

This can look unsightly unless carried out very carefully. However, it does have one virtue; it hides any pipes that have to be run down the side of the house from a kitchen or bathroom, although it is better to sink these partly into the soil or rock if this is a viable option.

As we have mentioned before, I'm a great advocate of PVA as it does help to ensure optimum adhesion under hot, dry Spanish conditions. We always keep a pot of 1:3 dilution by our side, with a brush inside, ready for use. With PVA you need have no worries about rendering over existing concrete, or even over areas of sound masonry paint if chipped to provide a better key. And if you work some PVA into the outer limits of any areas of render, these can be feathered out with the minimum risk of cracking. *TIP: we find full-strength PVA difficult to dissolve, so we always dilute the original can with 10% water from the outset. Further dilution is then much easier.*

Wall coatings

If you have difficulty in matching new and old walls, both areas can be coated with a textured finish as a last resort. Various specialist companies can carry out this work for you, or a local builder may have a hand-operated tool which flings a soft render mix on the wall. Be careful to ensure that such work is properly bonded to the wall and comes with a written guarantee; a badly applied coating can do more harm than good.

Spanish bricks

It won't be long before you have your first encounter with Spanish bricks. These come in a wonderful range of sizes, thicknesses, materials and uses, and they are very reasonably priced.

The normal type of building brick has six holes running along its length. These bricks have a number of advantages:

- They contain a large amount of air, so their insulating properties are good.

- They are much lighter to transport and handle.
- They can be strengthened, or even a simple lintel made, by passing reinforcing rod through them.

On the other hand:

- They are more fragile to use.
- It can be rather annoying to lay them and to render them as the mortar disappears down the holes of any ends which may be visible (but see the note below to avoid most of these).
- We have yet to master the art of halving them with a swift stroke of a bricklayer's trowel, so we always cut a few halves in advance with an angle grinder.

Some of these bricks have the holes running across their width. These are used on walls which are two bricks thick, for those "header" courses (usually about every fifth row) which span the width. The insulation properties are thus maintained and there are no ugly holes to be filled with cement render.

Sand-faced and other decorative bricks are only available from more specialised merchants and they are rather expensive. If you need a brick pillar—say for supporting a stoneware sink or bench in your kitchen or patio—it's more usual to use the common building bricks, render these and paint them white.

Rendering new brickwork

If the bricks to be rendered are perfectly dry, the cement mortar can be slightly more fluid than usual. However, when rendering the end of bricks with six holes, the render sometimes collapses into the holes. You could fill the holes first with a slightly stiffer mix, but this should not be necessary. By adjusting the stiffness of the render you should be able to avoid all but the occasional "blow hole". Avoid the temptation to apply too thick a coating. More than about a centimetre at the very most will begin to sag. Apply the render with an upward sweeping movement of a steel float, and even it off without delay. If you prefer a rustic finish, use a round-nosed gauging trowel for the final smoothing and aim for a slightly uneven finish. You may also find the plastering tips in the next chapter helpful.

Corners may present a problem as it is difficult to maintain their shape without the benefit of a plastering bead. One simple alternative is first to nail a piece of timber across one of the faces and render up to that. Remove it when the cement has set, and repeat the process. When rendering up against a doorway that is set back from the line of the wall, don't do the sloppy thing and round or angle the render back to it, but attach a strip of timber to the frame and render up to that so that you have a neat, square corner.

Mortar, concrete and PVA mixes

Hard cement mortar: for laying modern bricks, blocks or terracotta tiles only, or for small repairs:

1 part cement with plasticiser (or frothed-up washing-up liquid) in the mixing water

3 $^1/_2$ -4 parts sand —reduce to 3 parts if sand is very dusty

Hard render mix: for modern materials in exposed places, when bearing weight, when used in thin coats or for cementing harder bricks:

1 part cement with plasticiser (as above)

3 parts sand

Lime plaster/render: by far the best mix for stone laying and finishing, provided you can find the right materials:

3 parts fairly sharp building sand

1 part lime putty, made by adding quicklime to water and maturing for at least 3 months—see detailed instructions in next chapter.

Add hydraulic additive (pozzolan) for waterproofing if intended for external use or for internal waterproofing, according to instructions supplied with the product.

Cement/Lime mortar mix: only included for the sake of completeness, as building lime (i.e. slaked lime powder as opposed to raw lump quicklime) doesn't appear to be used very often in Spain. This mix is however useful for stone-laying or masonry rendering in exposed places; it is better than basic sand-cement mortar, but not in the same class as a putty-lime based mix as regards flexibility and permeability:

1 part cement (*cemento*)

1 part building lime

6 parts sand (*arena*)—reduce to 5 parts if sand is very dusty

For greater flexibility but reduced weatherproofing, amend proportions to 1:2:9.

Concrete mix: mixed ballast (small pebbles plus sand) is normally used as the basis for this, but it comes in a wider range than is often offered elsewhere. The full range can include very sharp (coarse) sand, fine or coarse chippings (usually white in colour), and fine, medium or coarse mixed ballast. Each has its use, and you should observe what local builders use for which purpose before ordering. The ideal proportion of cement to ballast will differ in each case, and even from one sample to another, so it is important to experiment with each new batch. As a general guideline, using a medium mixed ballast, we tend to use about 6:1 to 5:1 (ballast:cement) for sub-floor use, and $4^1/_2$ or even 4:1 when greater strength is required. This may sound a little on the extravagant side, but cement is not expensive in Spain.

Note 1: Spanish sand is of variable quality, and often contains quite a high proportion of fine dust. You may need to increase the amount of cement to compensate. On the other hand, the building sand may also include larger particles which tend to balance this out. Always carry out a preliminary test with every new batch of sand before cementing large areas; allow it to dry and check its strength.

Note 2: At the time of writing, bags of Spanish cement are being reduced from 50kg to 40kg in weight, but this is still heavier than the 25kg bags sold in more Health and Safety-conscious countries. Take great care when lifting them, and preferably seek help from the builder's merchant.

Note 3: We have found that some Spanish-made cement mixers rotate in a less horizontal position than we were used to, probably because Spanish builders prefer to mix mortar by hand in a large, square box using a hoe-like tool. As a result, although these machines are fine for mixing concrete, cement mortar never moves around properly unless it's on the verge of being too sloppy. The answer is to cut an extra notch or hole in the control wheel, to allow a slightly more horizontal motion. Note that this tends to place a greater strain on the drum bearing, and may invalidate the warranty, so reduce the total load accordingly. And *never* re-start the motor when fully loaded.

Note 4: Lime putty mortar must be kept damp for two to three weeks after application, to avoid cracks developing, during which time it undergoes the chemical transformation into a unique strong but flexible, waterproof yet permeable substance. The techniques for preparing lime putty, and whitewash paint, are described in Chapter 7.

PVA dilutions

We have recommended the use of PVA throughout this book, as so much building work involves cementing stones or rendering over concrete—neither of which can be reliably carried out without using this invaluable bonding agent. Strangely enough you may have difficulty in tracking down a supply, in which case you can substitute the largest available size (for the sake of economy) of the PVA wood glue, or Cola Blanca (not the waterproof version, though).

As a surface sealant: to seal cement surfaces (bare concrete etc) against producing dust—one or two coats at 1:4 (PVA:water).

For cement and plaster bonding (to ensure a proper bond between cement or plaster and stone or concrete): seal and bond with 1:3, using two coats if necessary. Allow to become tacky before cementing or plastering.

As an additive to plaster or cement render: dilute 1:1 and mix with the dry plaster or sand/cement powder; this gives exceptional adhesion and strength and is recommended in problem areas of extreme importance.

A standard mix of 1:3 stored in a sealed container can be kept on hand for the more common uses.

A mixer is almost essential if you intend to carry out much repair work, particularly flooring which seems to consume vast quantities of concrete mix. Constructing our patio needed 37 barrow-loads, for instance, which Erna valiantly mixed while I spread and consolidated. Prices of locally made mixers are quite reasonable.

Making your own lime putty or limewash (whitewash)

Ready-made lime putty (sometimes called putty lime) is not readily available in Spain. The reason for this is that most Spanish finca owners make their own. Quicklime is sold by most large builders' merchants, often in quite a coarse rocky form. This must be slaked, by adding it to water, and left to mature before use.

The techniques for slaking lime, adding various waterproofing compounds and preparing limewash for both internal and external use, is covered in the next chapter.

CHAPTER 7

THE INSIDE WALLS

The wall finish. Dealing with loose plaster. Rustic plastering technique. Damp walls. Penetrating damp. Rising damp. Damp floors. Permeable paints, traditional and modern. Distemper. Decorating tools. Making steps within internal walls. Converting an opening into an arch.

The wall finish

Older fincas which are likely to have been altered many times over possibly hundreds of years are likely to have a variety of internal wall finishes, even though they may appear similar at first glance.

It is important to scrape away a corner of each wall to investigate what lies beneath the surface, as the type of render or other finish used will determine how it should be redecorated. In our case we found rooms with examples of each of the following:

(1) In its most basic form, the bare stones had simply been painted with a thick lime wash, year upon year. This had built up to an appreciable thickness, but was still only a paint finish rather than a proper render. In many areas it was lifting away from the underlying clay, requiring more drastic action than most other rooms. This type of finish is more common in rooms that were originally built and used as animal shelters or stores rather than for human habitation. Because changes over the years may have involved converting an outside wall to a room interior, each wall should be assessed separately.

(2) Some walls had been covered with a lime/sharp sand render, sometimes with an underlying coat that included animal hair or even chaff. This was in better condition than the previous type, and often needed no repair before redecoration.

(3) Rooms that had received more recent attention, because of repairs or alterations, had been patched with a hard cement mortar. In some places this was both sound and dry, and these were either left as they were or lightly plastered before being decorated. Many areas, however, were hollow-sounding when tapped, and such areas had to be chopped out and re-rendered using a PVA mix to bond the new area in place.

(4) Walls that had been rebuilt in brick had been rendered in cement mortar—a perfectly normal and suitable treatment for such areas. These were redecorated in their original state, or after some superficial re-plastering, to blend in with the finish of other walls in the room.

We have already explained the risks involved in trying to cover a clay-based wall (particularly if it has inherent problems such as dampness) with a thin layer of hard cement rendering. Nevertheless, many people imagine that a lime plaster or paint finish is going to brush off against their clothing and leave a deposit on the floor following the occasional knock. So what is the truth of the matter, and how should your inside walls be treated?

Well, if a wall is sound and giving no problems, it's undoubtedly best to leave well alone before decorating it. Any attempt to wash or rub down the surface will disturb the countless layers of limewash that will have been applied over the years, and will give you extra work in patching and rectifying.

Unless it has already been painted with modern emulsion, we would generally advise against using this. Limewash (whitewash), and more recently distemper, are the traditional treatments, so why be the first to change things for the worse? Modern plastic emulsion paints are made to be washable, and that very feature implies very limited permeability which can trap the moisture inside your wall and store up problems for the future.

However, various finishes have fairly recently been introduced which incorporate a modern binder to give a durable surface while allowing the wall to breathe. It is encouraging to see that manufacturers are responding to this demand for practical paints that are suited to the needs of traditional walls, and it is worth keeping up-to-date with these developments through specialist paint suppliers or by contacting the technical departments of those manufacturers whose paints are most popular in your area. The Finca Book website includes a list of various specialist suppliers of modern, "breathable" paints and additives, which we will attempt to keep up-to-date.

Dealing with loose plaster

Loose plaster must be carefully removed, using a bricklayer's hammer or a scraper, the joints dug out where necessary and the wall primed with PVA before re-plastering (left). Apply the new surface with a float, and trowel it out to give a slightly uneven surface that matches that of the rest of the room (right).

Large areas of loose render or plaster usually indicate an underlying problem of dampness, which must be rectified before re-plastering (left). As the dampness had softened the surface of the bricks, they were chopped back and rendered (right) before re-plastering where necessary to match the finish on the rest of the wall.

If areas of lime plaster (or thickly applied layers of limewash) are already parting company with the wall, resist the temptation to hack it all off and re-plaster, as this will certainly destroy much of the character of your rooms. Instead, we suggest that you tap gently all over each wall, using a small block of wood. Each time you come across an area that sounds hollow, scrape away the surface plaster from that patch with a triangular scraper, or chop lightly with a small bricklayer's hammer, until you reach a firmer layer below. Sometimes you will only be scraping away countless layers of limewash paint that have accumulated over the centuries. In other places you may have to cut into the lime plaster beneath the paint layers, perhaps right back to the underlying stonework.

When this happens, check the condition of the underlying masonry. If this is decidedly damp, yet well protected from above, leave it open to the air for a while to help it to dry a little. Then you can repair this area, but this has to be done with care. Ideally, use a lime putty-sand mix plaster, using a moderately hydraulic additive that has improved waterproofing qualities, while still allowing the plaster to breathe and rid itself of future moisture.

Only if you are repairing or making good around a new window or door, where extra strength is needed, would we suggest you should automatically use a conventional sand/cement mortar on the inside of an external wall—but then that this area (if not the entire room) must be painted with distemper, rather than with straight limewash.

If any internal walls are becoming really crumbly and cannot be stabilised in any other way, and provided the wall behind is showing no signs of dampness and the area not too vast, they can also usually be repaired by raking out the failing clay or lime mortar quite deeply and carefully rendering with cement mortar. It is usually best to avoid applying modern plaster directly on to a clay-mortar wall, particularly if this shows any signs of inherent dampness, as the plaster will soak up any residual moisture in the wall like a wick, remain soft and give endless problems in future.

If your finca has previously been repaired in recent years, you will probably find that the internal walls have been finished in cement render, and not plastered at all. This is quite usual, and stems from the fact that any slight trace of dampness can quickly spread through plaster, whereas cement (while not waterproof) is better at holding it back. You may decide against plastering over such surfaces, but you should then remember to rub down the wall surface with medium glasspaper before painting, to remove the sand particles on the surface which will otherwise protrude through then thin layer of paint.

Rustic plastering technique

I—Alec—have to confess that I am no plasterer. In fact, an expert plasterer would weep at some of my work. I can produce a passable imitation of a polished finish when working in sections of a wall between battens, but freehand work is something I normally leave to the professional.

Fortunately this is no disadvantage when working on old fincas, where a perfect finish would look entirely out of keeping. For such purposes I have developed a technique which, while unconventional, is extremely effective at producing the desired "rustic" finish. As I have already explained, plastering should only be carried out if you are sure that the wall is perfectly dry, such as walls which have been extended or rebuilt using modern bricks and cement. On old walls which are in need of attention, yet which you do not wish to repair with lime putty plaster (possibly because part of the room is already cement rendered), you must first patch and resurface these areas using cement render. However, the general technique is quite similar.

With plaster, use the slower-setting yeso—often described on the bag as YG/L (L for *lento*)—or an equivalent, and mix it (plaster into water, never the reverse) to a smooth consistency slightly thicker than cream. The wall surface should be perfectly dry and any crumbling areas should first be raked out or primed.

The tool which you will be mainly using is the float, and this may be of steel, plastic or wood. The steel gives the smoothest finish, the others give a slightly matt surface, but in this case you will be brushing or sponging over the surface afterwards and so either can be used. Don't use too large a float, as you need to follow the irregularities and contours of the wall to some extent.

Scoop a trowel-full of plaster on to the back of a steel float, push it into contact with the bottom of the wall, and sweep the float upwards and diagonally across the wall with an even pressure to maintain a consistent thickness of coat. Repeat until you have covered a couple of square metres, merging each float-full with the previous one. Within a minute or two the plaster will start to set, and you must then work on it to achieve a smooth, but rustic, finish. This is done with a wide paintbrush (I use an old wallpaper pasting brush) that is occasionally dipped into a pot of dilute PVA. If you used water alone, the diluted and re-worked plaster would dry with a powdery finish. Pay particular attention to the corners of the area being worked, "feathering" them out to a thin coating so that they merge with the surrounding wall. Avoid using too much PVA as this may reduce the permeability of the plaster.

This technique is ideal in rooms with an already uneven finish, but there are some areas where the "rustic" finish simply won't do—particularly where the wall is to be tiled. Here, you apply the plaster as before, allow the plaster to become partially set, splash or spray a little water on to it and scrape it level with a metal straightedge or a straight piece of planed timber. Finally, add more water and work the surface to a polish with the float. This requires a little more practise but it is not as difficult as it is made out to be.

Finally, if you are really, really bad at plastering, and you don't manage to achieve a flat surface by the method above, there are various ways in which you can cheat. Let it dry thoroughly, then scrape down any high spots with one of those clever Surform hand files made by the Stanley tools people—I use the very smallest one known as a "Shaver" for this purpose; alternatively, coarse glasspaper can be used. Now check the flatness with a straight edge and fill any remaining holes with filler; a widely available brand in Spain is known as Aguaplast, and you need to look for the "Standard" type, which can be applied up to 5mm thick (or there's a *Capa Gruesa* version if you have deeper holes to fill). A final quick rub down with fine glasspaper on a sanding block will produce a smoother finish than you ever thought possible!

Damp walls

Damp patches fairly high up on the outside wall of a room can often be traced back to an outside timber lintel, as it is difficult to seal the joint around it. Usually the problem can be remedied by cutting out the joint more deeply and filling with a flexible waterproof medium such as *caucho* paint or exterior mastic sealer, prior to repainting. Small shrinkage cracks in cement beneath the joint between a wall and a ring beam, or around the top of a wall to which a modern roof has been fitted, can also be dealt with in a similar way. Alternatively they can be chopped out more deeply and filled with a waterproof cement mortar mix.

Severe water penetration

Occasionally you may come across a really damp wall in one of your rooms, leading to actual water penetration, as we did in one instance.

This room, which we chose for our bedroom (cool, north facing and low-set) had in fact been cut into the mountainside so deeply that the ground level along one wall was even higher than the ceiling. This made it delightfully cool in summer but it remained slightly damp after a month of airing, and even admitted a trickle of water after one severe downpour. It was obvious that the offending wall would need to be specially treated before it could be finished and decorated.

If at all possible, try to solve a problem like this at source. This may involve lowering the outside soil level, or tracing and blocking off the source of water. This was not an option in our case as there was no way we could dig away eight feet of solid rock.

In cases like this, we would ideally render the inside of the wall with a medium to strongly hydraulic lime, mixed with sand. Hydraulic lime is a unique compound that is capable of setting underwater, after which it resists the passage of water yet allows the moisture in the underlying wall to continue drying out.

It is hard to find a supply of this compound in Spain and you might have to ship some out from your home country. This would only be worth doing if you travel back and forth by car. If you normally fly, a more sensible alternative would be to slake your own lime in Spain (following the detailed instructions given later in this chapter), and buy in your home country only the additive that produces the waterproof properties. It is available in powder form.

Treating serious damp problems

Only if you have a severe problem with penetrating damp, and no way of obtaining the special hydraulic lime, should you consider any type of process that involves sealing off the inside of the room, as the dampness inevitably remains trapped within the wall to creep upwards indefinitely. It is therefore essential to take special precautions to allow this retained moisture to evaporate from the area immediately above the treated patch, as we will explain later.

However, if the wall effectively consists of the bare rock, rather than built up using stones and clay, it is unlikely to be adversely affected by sealed-in moisture (which can disperse underground during the dry season). In cases like this, the process can do nothing but good. Many of the oldest fincas contain at least one room which is cut deeply into the ground in this way, and this is the way to cure the inevitable damp problem.

The technique involves creating a waterproof membrane built up of several layers of rubberised paint, which is then protected and given a better appearance by covering it with plaster. The locally available waterproofing paint, available in various brands and generally known as caucho, can be used.

The photographs show this treatment in use in one of our rooms which had been dug 2.5 metres down into the rock; the method described is the standard technique for a British-made compound known as *Synthaprufe*, which we actually used as we had brought some out to Spain, as we were told that the nearest stockist is in Gibraltar. It occurred to us that *caucho* can be used in exactly the same way, and an experiment seemed to confirm this.

1. Hack off all crumbling render and plaster, back to a firm base, cutting well back into any loose clay mortar.

2. Then apply a sealing coat of PVA diluted 1:3 to these areas.

3. When dry, brush PVA diluted 1:2 over these areas.

4. While still tacky, render these treated areas with 3:1 sand/cement, to about 5mm below surface level.

5. Brush on two thick coats of rubberised waterproofing paint , allowing each to dry for 24 hours.

6. Apply the final coat of waterproofing, and then it must be "blinded" while still tacky by throwing sharp sand on with some force so that it sticks and forms a key for the plaster.

7. When this final coat is dry (another 24 hours), brush diluted PVA around the edges of the treated area for about 15cm, but not on top of it.

8. Now plaster with "YG/L" (i.e. the slow-drying version) mixed with water to a fairly thick but still creamy consistency. Apply with a float if you want a perfectly flat surface, or a round-nosed gauging trowel if the rest of the wall is also less regular. Do not make the plaster mix too runny, as the waterproofed wall offers little "suction" which would help to dry it out as it is applied. If the plaster sags, it is either too wet or you are try-ing to apply too thick a layer in one go.

9. Sponge with water when starting to set (normally about 20-30 minutes), removing any trowel marks. "Feather" the extreme outer edges into the surrounding area using a wide brush which has been treated with PVA. It is sometimes easier to brush on some diluted PVA before, or instead of, sponging, which then mingles with the plaster to give extra strength and to aid its adhesion.

10. Allow to dry thoroughly—which may take up to three weeks— before decorating. Do NOT seal the wall above the treated area with emulsion or other plastic-based paint but use distemper or similar water-permeable paint only. *This is very important.*

Only in rare, extreme cases should you need to seal a damp wall—in this case it is well below the outside soil level and the outer wall consists of natural rock rather than stone and clay. This picture shows the stage at which the treated wall, "blinded" with sharp sand, is ready to accept the plaster. This is being applied with a trowel rather than a float in order to achieve a slightly uneven finish that matches the rest of the room.

A variation of this technique can be used to seal a damp floor. The procedure is similar but of course the final covering is then of sand and cement screed, rather than plaster; or you can simply use a waterproofing additive, as used for swimming pools, in the screed itself.

Rising damp

Sometimes the cause of a damp wall may be difficult to spot and may arise from a problem area quite some distance away.

One of our walls was permanently damp, to the point where some of the bricks were crumbling away, yet it was not caused by penetrating dampness from behind. It was only after we lifted the floor that we discovered the rain falling off the roof was creeping beneath the front door and soaking along several metres of porous sand-and-cement beneath the floor tiles before creeping up the wall. Removing the rain-trapping front step, and laying a harder sub-floor, soon cured the problem.

Replacing the "modern" hard floor tiles with the traditional terracotta type also helped disperse any residual dampness by evaporation. We have to admit that it was very satisfying to discover and cure a problems like this which had defeated previous owners, despite the numerous measures they had obviously tried.

If the dampness really is serious rising damp (which is rare, and must indicate an underground aquifer), that is more difficult to treat. The usual remedy of cutting away sections of wall and inserting a slate or plastic damp-proof course is hardly possible when the wall is so thick, neither is an injected silicone solution likely to penetrate deeply enough, and you should seek the advice of a damp-proofing specialist who may suggest electrolytic inserts.

Traditional and modern types of permeable paint

The traditional finish for Spanish walls was limewash (whitewash) from around the 17th century, partly displaced by distemper when this was introduced. Both of which have the useful ability to allow moisture to escape and evaporate. This feature also has a small but useful effect of cooling the room during the evaporation process, as well as avoiding any problems from the rising damp that is inevitable when—as is usual—no damp-proof barrier has been incorporated into the base of the wall. If your walls have always been limewashed in the past, this same paint should be your first choice for regular redecorating, or you may apply distemper on top if you prefer.

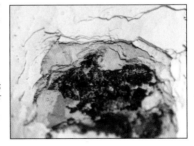

The walls of an old finca reflect its history when the scores of layers of limewash are revealed, right down to the rock and clay construction.

Preparing lime and making whitewash

Ready-prepared lime putty is rarely sold in Spain. Instead, you need to ask at the builder's merchant for *cal*, the raw lumps of quicklime. These are slaked (i.e. converted into lime putty) by adding them slowly to cold water in a bucket or barrel. Cal is normally stored in the cement/plaster section of your builder's merchant, in heavy duty plastic sacks, and this product must be handled with care.

The slaking process is potentially hazardous as the raw product is corrosive, with an extremely alkaline pH of around 13. When preparing and applying, you should take precautions to protect eyes and exposed skin. Many books warn you to wear rubberised clothing, aspirator and goggles, and this makes sense, particularly if a large quantity is being made. I must admit I didn't use this protective gear personally, but then I was working outdoors and dealing with fairly small quantities. We advise you to be more cautious as there is always the chance of a mishap. Whatever precautions you decide to adopt, the most important rules are to wear heavy rubber gloves when handling the quicklime, never work with bare arms or legs, and add a small amount at a time to cold water (never the other way round).

Allow plenty of water as the lumps of quicklime swell up considerably. Fill the container no more than two-thirds full of water, and add the lumps one at a time, stirring gently and carefully. Some users recommend using warm water to start the process off more reliably, but that calls for even greater caution. After you have added several lumps, the process will become more rapid and the liquid will warm up considerably, bubbling with gas and looking as if it is boiling. When you have finished and the mixture has cooled, add extra water so that there is a good layer of clear liquid on the top. Allow this to stand, preferably for at least three months before use, although we have found it can be used after only three or four weeks for painting purposes. You then scoop up what you need with a ladle, and either mix it with water (and a binder if required) to produce a limewash or add sand (and any waterproofing additive if required to make a mortar. Always store the remaining mixture beneath a layer of water, and keep it well covered to keep it clean and prevent it from drying out.

This whole process may sound rather long and involved, but it's worth it, which is why the same technique is still used to this day, despite the introduction of ready-made synthetic products. You can find more information in various web pages, and in several books which you may be able to borrow from the library. Your supply of slaked lime can be stored for several years in a plastic barrel, provided care is taken to ensure that it does not dry out.

Making limewash (whitewash)

To make limewash paint you can simply dilute the slaked lime with around six parts of water to the consistency of thick cream; use a paint stirring paddle on an electric drill to ensure a thorough mix, but wear goggles to keep any splashes from your eyes. This simple recipe gives quite a resistant finish but it can tend to rub off under hard pressure, so various additives can be used to make it more durable and rub resistant. If you enjoy experimenting, you will find numerous formulae on the internet which involve adding small quantities of raw linseed oil, casein (often added in the form of skimmed or goat's milk), tallow, molasses, flour, waterglass, soap or even flour, often in combination with about an ounce of alum per five gallons to assist dispersal. More modern acrylic additives can also be tried, as described later. Many of these additives will also make the limewash suitable for exterior use. It is sometimes recommended to apply limewash to a pre-dampened surface, and several coats are likely to be needed.

Lime-based paint or plaster has a wonderfully pure white finish. As the lime dries, which is quite rapid in the case of paint but which should be delayed for several days by spraying with water if applied in the form of lime plaster, it undergoes a chemical reaction which increases its water resistance and durability, which makes it a quite unique substance. Lime-based wall finishes are of course far cheaper than emulsion paint—although we must add that distemper is also remarkably inexpensive, in case you may decide to use that instead.

Old houses were regularly repainted throughout with lime-wash every year or two, the layers bonding together and building up in thickness to give what was effectively a lime render, lasting hundreds of years. In our case, we measured this layer to have reached an amazing 17mm thick and around forty of the coats could be separately counted, some of them tinted with various earth pigments.

Not only does a coating like this allow any moisture in the wall to evaporate, but its strong alkalinity inhibits mould growth and has other disinfecting and insect-repellent properties.

Flaking paint problems

You may encounter the common problem of blistering and flaking paint on outside walls, which is both unsightly and difficult to remedy. Sometimes the problem is due to rising or penetrating dampness, which must first be treated. But usually these patches occur where a modern plastic paint has been applied over areas which were cement rendered and then limewashed at some time in the past. There is no point in re-applying limewash, as this will not be happy on top of cement and will itself flake off before long. You could try an initial coat of "Stabilising Solution" (a special primer intended for soft and dusty surfaces) followed by a modern paint, but this is not always effective. We have found that the best answer is to scrape away the new paint from all around the problem area, and then scrub the remaining traces of lime from the bare patch with a mild acid (even vinegar might work), wearing rubber gloves to protect your hands. Wash the wall with clean water, leave for a week or two to dry out thoroughly, and re-apply the modern paint (the first coat being well diluted), which will then adhere properly.

Some of the most recently introduced lime-based paints incorporate a mild acrylic binder, and earth pigments are added for colouring if required. The acrylic is accepted in conservation circles as a replacement for traditional tallow or casein. It seems to give a more durable result without losing the original properties of limewash, and it is non-toxic and sweet smelling (the unpleasant odours in emulsion paints come from other chemical ingredients). It does restrict the permeability a little, but the result is a very reasonable compromise. However, you will need to find a specialist supplier for this type of additive.

Distemper—worth trying indoors

Unfortunately, difficulties are often encountered after applying limewash paints on to areas of cement render or even modern gypsum-based plaster, even when primed with PVA or with a weak, 20% mixture of lime putty in water. Some of the modern hybrid lime paints incorporating an acrylic binder are more tolerant in this respect, but another good alternative to use is distemper paint, which is easier to obtain as it is has been used to redecorate the interiors of Spanish houses for over a hundred years.

There are few surfaces on which distemper cannot satisfactorily be used: lime putty plaster, hard gypsum plaster or even over matt emulsion paints. If your walls are likely to contain areas of different materials, distemper is the safest paint to use. It is available in a wide range of colours, and shouldn't be hard to find. Ask for *pintura al temple*; often, as in the trade brand Colamina which we used, it is supplied in polythene bags as a thick paste needing further dilution.

Using slightly warm water and a paint-stirrer attachment on your electric drill will speed up the process. Stir for about five minutes with the stirrer head held just below the surface of the paint at an angle of 45 degrees. We find that one of the larger 25kg bags of this will just fill a 15 litre paint tin when diluted for use. It should have a creamy consistency, just slightly thicker than modern paints, although the first coat on bare plaster can be thinned to act as a primer. Unlike emulsion paint (the smell of which we loathe) distemper has virtually no odour. It keeps well, is quick to apply and can be removed very easily from brushes, hands, clothes, and even hair, using water alone.

When applied and still wet, distemper is pale pearl grey in colour and is surprisingly transparent (the underlying surface shows through quite clearly), but it dries to a pure white with a quite unexpected covering power. Distemper, unlike limewash, shows up any damp patches underneath in a pale grey, which is a helpful indicator of any problem areas needing future attention.

Distemper can be coloured using liquid pigments (of which a wide range is readily available, although we find the resulting colours tend towards pastel tones) or with natural earth powder pigments such as terracotta, ochre and raw umber (available from a few specialists, listed in the book's own website, www.finca-book.com, and these give a more solid feel to the result. In our sitting room (the one with the delivery hatch in the wall), we matched the original golden brown colour very successfully by using Golden Ochre from a company called Rose of Jericho. The colour you obtain will naturally vary according to the concentration of the pigment, so always mix enough to cover the whole room (and keep a small pot in reserve for touching up) or you may have difficulty in matching it exactly.

It can be helpful to keep a small pot of thicker distemper mixture handy, as this can be used to fill any small cracks and holes in the wall as you paint. You will find that any areas of the original wall-building clay which are close to the surface are inclined to "bleed" through the distemper to give a brown stain, even after applying several coats, so you should check for these before you begin and ensure that they are first covered in lime putty, rendered over with cement or sealed with any impervious paint.

Distemper does, however, have a few limitations. It cannot be washed or subjected to any source of dampness, so it may be unsuitable for inside windowsills if there is any danger of rain blowing in. Around the kitchen sink is another area which you will need either to tile or apply emulsion paint. Distemper will also wash off along the floor line if a tiled floor is washed, so you should either fit a narrow skirting board or—the usual Spanish method—paint a narrow strip of gloss paint around the walls at just above floor level.

Spanish emulsion paints sold specially for internal use work satisfactorily if the walls are completely dry. However, a paint can be "moisture vapour permeable" yet still seal the surface to a degree that can prevent any substantial amount of rising moisture from escaping (external masonry paints may fall into this category), so check with the manufacturer's technical helpline. It has been said that modern paints cannot be used on any wall in which the moisture content is above 6%, and this includes most walls built without a damp-proof course, or using a clay mortar, no matter how hot the climate.

Don't be afraid to experiment, though. For example, you might decide that by adding 25% of matt emulsion to distemper, you achieve the ideal compromise between durability and permeability. Most water-based paints are inter-mixable, but don't go overboard or you may end up with a hybrid that combines the disadvantages of all its components while lacking any of their benefits.

To summarise

Let us summarise this matter of choosing and applying paint as an unwise decision may limit your future options. Slight dampness is inevitable in some parts of an old finca. You cannot expect simply to paint over such areas with any type of modern waterproof paint or sealer. If you do, this layer will eventually flake off. Instead, you must either totally cure the dampness at source, which can involve major surgery, or—if less serious—you can paint with either limewash or distemper, through which the moisture can harmlessly evaporate.

Of these two alternatives, distemper can be applied to any surface, including cement render and modern plaster, although areas which are permeating water vapour may appear slightly grey (but at least it doesn't flake off within a few weeks, as emulsion would). Limewash can only be applied directly on to a lime plastered wall, on which surfaces it is unquestionably the best choice, but you will need to prepare your own. Neither distemper nor limewash should rub off on your clothes, but they are definitely not washable and any splashback areas should be treated differently (and possibly tiled).

Re-decorating tools

We have mentioned before the advantages of using certain Spanish tools and utensils, and paintbrushes are a good example. Those round, colourful brushes which they use when painting the walls are excellent, being both inexpensive and practical. Being round, the brush can be wielded in any direction, which is useful when painting uneven stonework, and they seem to hold quite a lot of paint in reserve. They are also good for working thicker lime paint into crevices and producing a good, even finish.

The innermost wall of a finca can be 3 to 4 metres high and can be difficult to reach, so buy the largest stepladder you can find. High walls can also be tackled with a paintbrush on a telescopic handle, both parts of which are readily available. Brushes are available which have a thread inside the end of their plastic handle, into which you screw the end of the telescopic handle. These are fine to a point but they cannot work at a very steep angle before the side of the brush rubs against the wall. Paint rollers have no such limitation as they can be used with the handle almost flat against the wall. And these are also available in versions with the threaded insert to suit the extension handle. Choose the types with a rough fleecy finish designed for masonry work—the smooth wool or foam types are only intended for use on flat walls.

Constructing steps within a wall

Many old fincas were built on a hillside, as was our *lagar*, and this means that each adjacent room is several steps up or down. Whenever you extend into an adjacent area, bear in mind that there may be a substantial difference between the level on either side of the wall, and bore a pilot hole to ascertain this in advance, taking care to ensure that the drill and/or chisel you use is held perfectly horizontal and at right angles to the surface for an accurate indication. In one instance when I foolishly omitted to drill a test hole, the ground level on the other side of the door proved to be over 90cm higher than the room I was in. Fortunately this was easily overcome as the wall was almost a metre thick at that point, allowing the necessary steps to be built largely within it.

The combined effect of thick walls and a steep mountain can produce a considerable difference in levels between adjacent rooms—almost a metre in this case, so that the door looks more like a window (left). Most of the necessary steps can usually be built within the thickness of the wall, as here (right). The top step is shallower because the outside courtyard is being built up.

Whether or not the steps can be contained within the wall will be decided by various factors, but principally by the slope of the ground which gives rise to the difference in level. Steps that are comfortable to climb will have an equivalent average slope of no greater than 40 degrees, equivalent to 22cm treads and 17cm risers. If you find that you would need to climb more steeply than that, you can do two things:

(a) Extend the bottom step out into the room.

(b) Chop the top step out of the upper room.

It is not uncommon for existing steps, which were constructed years before any regulations came into force, to be quite steep. Ours had risers of 25cm each, compared to the usual 18cm maximum. The wall may be so thick that several steps can be incorporated within it, but always make sure there is sufficient headroom at the highest point. This may involve having a sloping ceiling to the opening in the wall.

Steps can be built of bricks, or they may be cast in concrete. Bricks are quicker to lay and can be altered more easily, but they are more easily damaged and lack the solidity of concrete, which can even be poured on to a rough, sloping rock base. Which ever you decide to use, always build the bottom step first, and work upwards so that the front of the second step rests on the back of the first one. When calculating the dimensions, allow for the thickness of any tiles you might wish to lay on top of the steps.

Building new steps on bedrock

1) Clear the area down to solid rock, as here, and prime with 25% PVA solution. The steps themselves are often made from bricks, but when building on to sloping bedrock it is better to construct shuttering and fill with concrete.

2) *Decide the dimensions of each tread and riser by dividing the total width and height by the number of steps. If each step is higher than about 7in (175mm) and narrower than about 9in (225mm), consider increasing the total width by cutting back into the upstairs room and/or protruding into the lower one. Both methods were needed here as the total rise was so great. Then construct a shuttering box for the bottom step using 25mm thick timber planks.*

3) *When the concrete in the bottom step has set, add the shuttering for the next step up—in this case the front was level with the wall surface. Repeat the process until the job is completed, then render the sides. If the cut sides of the wall need filling by more than about 2cm thick, use shuttering and fine concrete mix instead. Then make good the other joints, and finally tile the steps.*

93

Forming an arch in a wall

Sometimes you need permanent open access between rooms, and it may be more appropriate to build it in the form of an arch. Forming this is often left to a builder but it's a job which you can tackle yourself if you have average DIY skills.

The first step is to make your own former out of 9mm ply or MDF; the photographs show this being made and used. Saw out two semi-circles, of the same diameter as the door opening, one for each side of the opening. Pin and glue into place between the two circumferences short lengths of 25x12mm timber, each piece being of the same length as the thickness of the wall, to be fitted at 10cm intervals. Cover the curved area with a continuous layer of whatever you can find—thin ply or tin sheet are best. Attach this arch former in place with two overlapping lengths of 50x25mm timber along each wall, and wall-plugged into place. Infill the gaps with bricks, chopping into the side walls to give a good bond, and using a strong mortar of about 3 parts of sand to one of cement. When this has set, render and plaster.

Converting an existing doorway

Make a former as described above. To provide greater strength, you should—at the lower point of the arch on each side—chop out the existing wall by the width of a brick, so that the new arch effectively rests on the old brickwork. The entire assembly is fitted to the opening, either by supporting it with props from below, or by timber battens each side plugged into the wall, and the first course of the new brickwork is commenced with each brick at a radial angle. Infill, render and plaster over as above.

Simply infilling an existing opening provides little structural support for brickwork above the opening as you are relying for strength on a horizontal grip. Such an arrangement is only acceptable if there is an existing lintel which will be left in position, or if the wall finishes at the top of the arch. Even so, care must be taken to key the new infill into the vertical opening, such as by use of brick ties, galvanised frame brackets or by occasional notching into the wall, otherwise all the new work could simply drop downwards!

We would stress that the arch which we made and described was perfectly able to support the wall above, but nothing more—it could not be properly described as load-bearing. To construct an arch within a wall which supports an upstairs floor or roof structure is a job for the professional.

The partially constructed arch former, showing how it is made from braced sides of MDF with the left-hand half already covered with thin ply.

Fitting the former within the existing opening, where it is secured in place with timber battens plugged into the side walls.

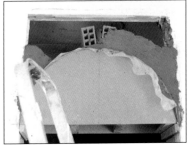

The first course of bricks helps to spread the weight above. These should be fairly thin, evenly spaced and firmly cemented with fresh 3:1 mortar. The plastic liner prevents the dampness from warping the wood.

Such an arch, in which an existing opening is infilled, offers little load-bearing strength. This was improved by adding new pillars and a further arch to the other side of this thin wall (seen here before completion and rendering), the first course being common to both sides. The centrally pivoted wire was used as a guide when rendering.

Finally, infill, render and plaster flush with the edges of the former. Remove the former after two days by unscrewing the battens, and plaster the inside of the arch. This shows the finished result, including the steps beneath.

CHAPTER 8

ABOVE ALL, THE ROOF

Typical roof construction. Checking the beams. If you need new beams. Looking after old beams. Techniques for re-roofing without losing character. Concreting and plastering a bamboo ceiling to make an upstairs room. Decorating the ceiling. Ring beams. Dealing with leaks. Guttering. Roof loading. Chimneys and flues.

Typical roof construction

In the more common type of roof construction, the roof is supported on sloping beams of eucalyptus or chestnut, about 10cm to 15cm in diameter, each end being sunk about half-way into the front and back wall. The angle of slope varies from area to area, and it is important to ensure that yours remains the same if it is to blend in with the surrounding fincas. Eucalyptus is a hard, strong wood, fairly resistant to rot and insect attack, and identified by its characteristically grey-whitish appearance and a few sharply protruding knots. Any loose bark should have been removed from either type of wood before or when the house was built, otherwise an unsuspected woodworm attack can spread beneath the bark.

Only the smallest finca would have just a single span roof. Normally the higher wall also supports another sloping roof on the opposite side. One roof often peaks at a slightly lower level than the other, but even if the two roofs join at the same height there is still a central wall in place to support them: This makes the whole structure more stable, and avoids the need for a more complicated arrangement of roof beams.

Usually the roof beams (we would regard these as rafters) run unsupported from ridge to eaves, and we haven't encountered any instances of using a purlin across them to provide added support. The spacing of the beams varies considerably, according to the thickness and type of timber available at the time of construction. Often the narrower beams, spaced more closely together, were used to roof the animal quarters.

Across the top of the beams goes a layer of bamboo—not the thin or split variety often used for screening against sun and wind, but quite thick canes that are laid across the beams at right angles, and which are capable of bearing a surprisingly high load.

Next follows a thick layer of clay, in which the lower tiles or gutter tiles (*tejas de canal*) are embedded, followed by the inverted top tiles (*tejas superior or cobijas*) also set in clay. The lower ends overhang the walls to shed rain and the overhanging portion consists of a double layer to give the necessary support.

Ceilings were formed by binding bamboo canes across the beams. These are liable to harbour numerous insect pests and may need to be replaced or encased in cement and plaster.

In the oldest buildings, the bamboo is visible from beneath and often provides a home for an interesting variety of insect life. In recent years it has become usual to plaster over this bamboo between the beams to provide a more practical finish. This is not quite such a simple procedure as it might seem. For one thing the bamboo is quite uneven, and a compromise has to be reached between a smooth finish and an unreasonable thickness of plaster. Also, as the beams are round in section, care must be taken to avoid an over-large, ugly vertical wedge of plaster against the side of each beam. The technique is the same as that used on the underneath of flat ceilings beneath upstairs rooms, and is described later in that connection.

The main exception to this form of roof structure is found in the *Alpujarra* region (that slopes down from the Sierra Nevada to the Mediterranean coast in the province of Granada), where the roof is almost flat and the final waterproofing comes from a layer of a unique, locally found river-bed substance rather than tiles. This is cheaper to lay but it relies on local expertise which is gradually dying out, and the life of the roof is considerably less. We have only visited this area briefly but have the impression that most new building construction and, sadly, a high proportion of the renovation work on older fincas, is now carried out using more conventional techniques.

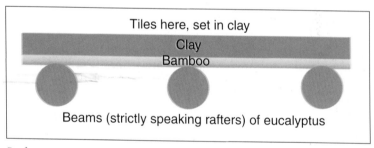

Roof construction—original type.

The modern roof is built in quite a different way, and can usually be identified by its perfectly straight slope with no hint of a dip. Between the two walls, concrete beams known as vigas are fitted. Into these are slotted fragile-looking, hollow terracotta oblongs known as *bovedillas*, which line up with the vigas above and below to give a smooth surface. On top, they are finished off with an upper layer of fine concrete before the original half-round tiles are replaced; worse still, interlocking modern pantiles are sometimes used instead. Beneath, the ceiling is plastered and becomes perfectly smooth. A similar basic structure can used for intermediate floors. *Bovedillas* give better insulation than *raciones*, but at higher cost. An alternative version was more recently introduced, made of expanded polystyrene.

Old roofs that need replacing can be identified by their distinct sag in the middle, often combined with broken tiles, washed-out clay and an abundant growth of weeds. When this stage is reached there is little that can be done to remedy the situation other than removing the tiles and replacing the beams.

Most builders, faced with a roof that needs replacing, will automatically opt for the modern arrangement. They will explain, quite justifiably, that it is cheaper, stronger and quicker to erect. However, there are ways of restoring a roof that incorporate the modern advantages of strength, weatherproofing and insulation, while retaining much of the original character.

If you try and persuade most builders to adopt this approach, you will invariably be told that this is *not* the correct way to do the job. If you want to see nice wooden beams, they will insist, you should add them beneath a modern roof as a cosmetic feature. We can only suggest that you obtain as many opinions as possible on your particular roof before coming to a final decision on this important matter.

If your repair work is likely to come under the close scrutiny of the planning department at the *ayuntamiento*, this may also influence your decision—although we gain the impression that they are usually more concerned with the strength and appearance of the finished job rather than the finer points of your restoration technique.

The one option which we have not considered—perhaps unfairly—is that of total authenticity. Bamboo is a remarkable material for the laths as it is both strong and flexible, but it does have drawbacks—particularly its limited life, and its attractiveness to undesirable insect life. Clay mud is also a remarkable building material if carefully maintained, but deterioration is fairly rapid once water does penetrate into it. If you are restoring animal quarters or a storage barn for fun, by all means adopt the authentic approach, but for habitable buildings we feel that some sort of compromise is desirable.

Check the beams

Before deciding which method to use, carry out a careful check of the beams for any signs of rot or worm attack. First try to force the blade of a knife into the grain at the point where each of them enters the wall. Any softness here indicates the onset of rot, and the beams will have to be replaced. Check them also for woodworm (tell-tale signs of course being holes in the surface). If you find any, cover some with a piece of clear tape, tap the wood, and see whether any dust sticks to the tape, indicating current or recent activity. Also make a rough check of the diameter of the beams, using a calliper or a couple of pieces of thin timber and a measuring rule across them, as a guide for ordering any replacements you may need.

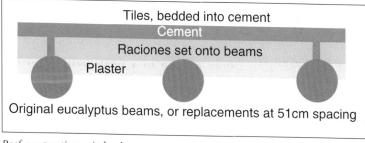

Roof construction—timber beams, new raciones above.

Two techniques

Assuming that the timber beams are sound and have only a minimal amount of dip, and if the bamboo beneath is free from serious rot and insect life, you have two choices. In each case you first remove and carefully stack the original tiles. Then, provided the beams are sufficiently thick—which may mean up to 9-10cm diameter according to span—the *raciones* can be laid over the top, each one being packed out to give a level top surface, before cementing over and replacing the original tiles. As the raciones are 1 metre across, it may be necessary to remove and re-lay the rafters at slightly over 50cms centre spacing (allowing for a cemented joint) to provide a stable base *(see Illustration 2)*.

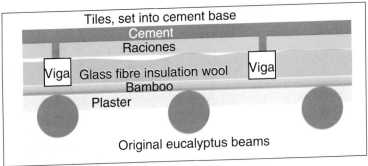

Tiles, set into cement base
Cement
Raciones
Viga   Glass fibre insulation wool   Viga
Bamboo
Plaster
Original eucalyptus beams

Roof construction—complete original roof with insulation and raciones.

Alternatively, a stronger method is to build up the walls a little and build in some new concrete vigas above the entire existing roof, with 10cm or 15cm of glass fibre insulation sandwiched between the two, before laying the raciones and finishing as before *(as in Illustration 3)*.

We chose this option when re-roofing our kitchen area, where we needed extra strength to hold the possible weight of a future solar heating panel and tank, and the improved insulation to keep the room cooler in summer and warmer in winter.

In each case, the usual technique for waterproofing is to paint the layer of fine concrete covering with two coats of red *caucho* rubber paint. This is not shown in either of the illustrations for the sake of simplicity. You may also prefer to spray the bamboo with insecticide before covering it in this way.

If you need new beams

Both of the above techniques offer the advantage that the original beams are undisturbed. It has been interesting to try each of them on different areas of our finca and compare the results. In older houses, these beams play an important role in tying the front and back walls together, and any risk of damage to the walls is reduced if you can leave the beams in place.

If, however, the beams are badly rotted, you will need to replace them—and it is worth mentioning that new timbers are available, but should be individually selected as they will form a feature of the ceiling. If you do the job yourself, and you have the time and patience to replace one at a time and then wait for the cement to set before progressing to the next, the chance of walls falling down is greatly reduced.

Showing the progressive construction of a new roof using timber beams rather than concrete vigas. The position of the ring beam on the side wall can also be clearly seen.

Finding good quality eucalyptus or chestnut roof timbers in Spain is far from easy. We did track down a good selection of imported, treated and untreated pine beams, at a place called *Maderas Aserraderos Velez*, in Velez-Málaga. Most timber merchants only seem to stock the machine rounded, green-treated poles which never look right.

If you do decide to replace your timbers, ensure that they are fitted at exactly 50-51cm centres. In that way you will be able to cover them with *raciones* exactly across the beams, joining at every second beam, just as if you were using the less attractive concrete *vigas*, at double the spacing, and build up the roof in the modern way without losing the rustic appearance indoors.

By the time the tiles are replaced, some will inevitably have been broken. Make sure your builder has allowed for the cost of replacing these in the estimate. More importantly, stress that all of the top tiles (the ones that show) should be original, or matching second-hand replacements, and that any new tiles must only be fitted to the bottom (gutter) layer where they will hardly show.

As we mentioned before, the bamboo can be left showing if you are a strict traditionalist, or it can be plastered over, pressing the cement render and/or plaster well into the gaps to provide a good key. Should *raciones* have been used to replace the bamboo, these should definitely be plastered underneath or you'll be left with your old farmhouse looking more like an industrial building.

We have already explained that we have areas of roof which have been replaced using each of these techniques, and after two years' weathering we have been assessing and comparing the results. The new concrete beams above the existing roof are fine. It's good to retain the original interior appearance and the insulation between the two has been a bonus, but the extra external height is noticeable outside, without any internal gain in space. The roof with new timber beams is structurally the best, we feel, but these pristine pine timbers lack the character of the originals. The new roof laid straight on to the original beams is a useful technique where the timbers are beefy enough to support the extra weight, but they do not look quite as solid as the re-timbered roof and only time will tell.

Looking after your beams

Roof beams were traditionally limewashed along with the walls and ceiling. This was not an ideal treatment as the limewash inevitably flakes away from the timber, but it did offer one major advantage: it provided a degree of protection against woodworm attack. You may not wish to hide your new (or, indeed, old) beams beneath a coating of lime, but some alternative protection must then be applied or the timber will be very vulnerable to attack. Sadolin Basecoat is a good general-purpose preservative, readily available, or you can apply a specific woodworm treatment and protection solution. The timber can then be left unpainted, or it may be further protected and enhanced with a suitable stain, clear varnish or paint.

Concreting over bamboo ceilings

You may have rooms with flat ceilings, consisting of horizontal beams with bamboo across them. Often the area above will have been used for storage of animal fodder. The bamboo harbours dust and numerous anti-social creepy-crawlies, and you may consider removing the bamboo or even doing away with the whole structure to leave the room open to the roof.

This is not always the best move. The room may be easier to keep warm in winter if it has a lower ceiling, and the space above could be useful—if only for dry storage or as a teenage den. If you are thinking of having a ring beam fitted (see later), which effectively raises the roof by about twenty centimetres, the headroom above may be improved to the point where the room can be used as a normal bedroom.

Provided the cross-beams are sufficiently sound and strong (and you might like to take advice on this point), you could leave the bamboo in place and encase it in concrete, sealing the fate of any insect pests and providing a sound floor. As a very rough guide, we would like to see 100mm diameter eucalyptus beams at no more than 45cm (18in) centres, or 125mm beams at 53cm (21in) centres as an absolute minimum before adding the weight of a concrete floor.

The ceiling needs to be reinforced with welded steel reinforcement, which is supplied in pieces measuring 2m x 6m, just about enough for a small room. This sheet can be rolled up loosely (with some difficulty) and carried on a car roof-rack to avoid incurring the delivery charge which most builders' merchants would otherwise add. After carefully straightening this rolled-up mesh, we attached it to the bamboo with pieces of wire, inserting 20mm thick pieces of tiles between the two as spacers. Any large gaps in the bamboo were covered with pieces of sacking or rags (or even, in a few cases where the gap was larger, using expanded steel mesh). We also bolted some heavy frame ties into the side walls at mid-concrete level, adding to the overall strength.

Laying reinforced concrete on a strongly built bamboo ceiling to form an upstairs floor. Note how the reinforcement is held centrally in the layer of concrete by inserting small pieces of tile.

When the concrete is dry, the underneath of the bamboo can be plastered using Yeso.

At this stage we also laid various sections of corrugated electrical conduit for the wiring which was needed in the upstairs room, as well as for some wall lights in the room below. Further pieces of conduit were added at points where future pipework was to pass straight up through the new ceiling.

Another useful preparatory job involved screwing a pulley wheel into a conveniently located strong roof beam, to aid the lifting of the many buckets of cement which were going to be needed.

The thickness of the concrete was regulated by placing small off-cuts of 30mm timber on top of the bamboo. We made a strong concrete mix, 4 parts medium (15mm) mixed ballast to one of fresh cement. Then we poured this mix on to the bamboo, tamping it down well and trowelling it out to an even thickness before smoothing the top with a steel float. The wet concrete effectively imposes a heavier load than after it has set, after which the steel reinforcing and stiff structure help to spread the weight; in certain cases it may be wise to carry out the concreting in sections, allowing 24 hours between each and binding adjacent sections together with PVA.

This thickness of concrete—say 25mm to 30mm—assisted by the bamboo and steel reinforcement is quite adequate for normal light use, but it's not the sort of floor on which you would want to hold a teenage rave, install a printing press or fill with heavy furniture! The thickness can be increased if necessary, but do not exceed the load bearing capacity of the beams and take advice on strengthening or replacing these if you are at all doubtful.

Plastering a bamboo ceiling

When the concrete has set, the underneath of the bamboo, between the beams, can be plastered. This is a job on which we almost gave up, as the plaster simply refused to stay in place over the shiny bamboo and seemed to delight in peeling away from one end of a strip just as we finished the other. So where were we going wrong? Partly because we were trying to use the "*lento*" (slower) version of *yeso*, which doesn't have quite as much grip as the rapid version.

Then we switched to the faster-setting type, but this seemed to become unworkable within about 30 seconds, heating up considerably in the process (the two types are very different). In the end we compromised with a mixture of rapid and slow versions, which stayed workable for a reasonable period but still stuck well enough. We also found that it was very important to ensure that the bamboo was free of dust, by peeling off any loose sheaths and then giving it a vigorous spray of water before plastering.

Decorating the ceiling

Many of our old ceiling beams had been lime-washed, and it seemed as if this had not incorporated any form of binding agent as it was flaking off. As far as we could see, there were only three options open to us:

* Scrub off the lime, allow to dry, and then stain the wood.
* Scrape off the very loose areas, paint with a stabilising primer and repaint with emulsion or oil paint.
* Engage a firm to sand blast the beams completely clean for us, then stain or clear varnish.

It seemed most sensible to try the first option first. This worked in one room where the limewash was thinly applied, but we decided to leave the timber unstained as the natural, slightly "limed" effect was so attractive. Elsewhere the original paint was less easily removed, and so the second choice was used. The final technique may be the only resort if the beams are covered in thick oil paint and you are desperate to have them stripped completely, but we ruled that one out on grounds of cost and mess.

As for the colour, there is a general rule that darker colours have the visual effect of lowering the ceiling, so it is often better to strip, stain or paint the beams a darker colour in very tall rooms, and to paint them white if the ceiling is low and you don't want to emphasise it.

Limewash does not take properly on wooden beams and any loose coating needs to be scraped off before sealing, staining or painting, as you prefer.

To ring beam or not to ring beam?

In cases where the entire roof needs to be removed, you will be offered the option of incorporating a ring beam (*hormigón armado*). This consists of a concrete strip cast in wood shuttering around the entire building, at eaves level, in which are embedded steel reinforcing rods. It can only be fitted if the entire roof and supporting beams are first removed, as it is set on top of the wall and normally entails raising the wall level by the height of the strip, which is about 15–20cm. This can be turned to your advantage if you have any upper rooms with ceilings just too low for convenience. The less acceptable (and probably unwise) alternative would be to "scalp" the top of each wall first, thus loosening the masonry and damaging any interior finish.

Opinion is divided as to the desirability of this structure. Claims made for it are that it reinforces the walls and prevents future problems, holding the corners in particular very efficiently, acting almost as a foundation in reverse and providing an excellent base for supporting the roof. It is fitted to a high proportion of restorations, so there must be something in it.

On the other hand, some surveyors cast doubts on the claims made for it. They point out the difficulty in maintaining the necessary high concrete strength specification under hot, dry conditions, and suggest that it may be unwise to impose a rigid structure on top of a naturally flexing, breathing wall. It's one of those instances where it's difficult to know whom to believe, as even the experts disagree.

We decided to go ahead with a ring beam on the greater part of our finca after carefully considering the advantages and drawbacks. The result looks very efficient, is fairly inconspicuous, and overall we feel that the extra cost was probably justified. It does offer the further advantage that you can usually chop out in order to fit a small upstairs window without worrying too much about a lintel, as it is effectively already in place across the entire top of the wall.

One occasional disadvantage of the ring beam is that it may leave a damp strip or a line of efflorescence inside the room, along the line where it joins the top of the wall. It is usually possible to seal this area before painting with a permeable finish, when the moisture can safely disperse around the surrounding area.

A ring beam may help to stabilise the walls, and consists of reinforcing rods encased within a concrete strip; the picture on the left shows the shuttering being fitted, with the finished result to the right (both photographs by John Sutherland-Hawes). This has the secondary effect of raising the roof slightly, which could be just sufficient to convert a low hay loft (below, left) into an occasional bedroom (below, right).

Dealing with leaks

When it rains in Spain it really can pour down, and most old buildings sprout the odd leak. Even after repairs have been carried out, you may still find the occasional trouble spot, particularly if existing features like chimneys have been retained. Other places to watch are roof junctions where there is a difference in level, the point where the power supply cable reaches the wall, and areas of new cement-work surrounding new doors and windows which have not yet been properly painted to seal them, or which may contain small shrinkage cracks.

Always remember that cement mortar and render may look hard enough but it is not actually waterproof. In areas where water lies on its surface, or runs across it in any quantity, the rain will eventually creep in. Exterior paint will help but it is not thick enough to cover every crack and pinhole. The answer lies in the waterproofing paint known as *caucho*. Available in red, white and clear versions, it is applied in a couple of successive coats and provides a completely waterproof barrier that is even suitable for swimming pools.

Guttering

Four months of virtually wall-to-wall sunshine make it easy to forget the need to channel torrential rainfall away from your walls. Rainwater is a valuable commodity and—being softer than most mains water—is useful for washing hair and clothes, apart from its obvious use in watering the garden, so it makes sense to conserve what you can. The rainwater can be stored in an underground tank, or in individual water butts, for use at a time of need. It is also a sound idea to divert rain from the front door area at least, to make it easier to enter on a pouring wet day and to reduce the risk of dampness running in beneath the door.

Spanish guttering tends to be of a larger size than is usual elsewhere, as it has to cope with a greater volume of water, and it is fairly expensive. A wide variety of fittings are available which make the system quite easy to attach, including a very useful type of gutter bracket which clamps on to the ends of the roof tiles. You may have difficulty in obtaining guttering and downpipes in a white finish (other than the outdated asbestos type) and you may have to settle for the rather incongruous grey plastic.

Roof loading

If you might be placing any great load on the roof, such as one of those solar heating panels which have an integral tank, it is wise to obtain professional advice. The traditional timber beam construction may be unable to bear such a weight, and you would be well advised to fit a new roof supported on concrete vigas. This can be fitted over the top of your existing ceiling (as explained earlier) if the extra roof height is acceptable and you want to retain the interior character.

Chimneys

Unless you intend to live in a favoured coastal area, you will need to heat your finca in winter despite the sunny climate. Central heating is becoming increasingly popular, and we can understand why. On one of our early visits to our finca at the beginning of May one year, we were looking forward to some warm sunny days, particularly as I'd been swimming in the sea during a visit three months earlier. Leaving a cold, unsettled Britain, and looking forward to something considerably better, we were alarmed upon arrival to find it wet, windy and a freakishly unseasonal 7 degrees!

If you are not considering central heating or properly fitted gas room heaters, you'll certainly need to incorporate a chimney or flue when designing the roof, as it is unwise (and expensive) to rely entirely upon electricity. But keep in mind that hot chimneys and roof timbers (especially if the original bamboo is still being used) are a potentially dangerous combination, so make sure there's a safe gap between the two. Boiler flue pipes are in fact usually taken out through the gable end wall, where it is easier to waterproof the point of exit.

Because our chimney starts well below the ridge, it had to be taller than normal in order to work efficiently. The design of the chimney top varies from region to region, and it's best to follow local tradition.

An open fire is a cheery, welcoming sight but in practice many finca owners complain that theirs is smoky and unusable under certain weather conditions. Building a new chimney is a skilled operation, and a short, straight chimney cannot be expected to perform well in all weathers, especially when the wind blows straight over the ridge.

It needs to be weather proof, to draw properly, to be adequately supported across the chimney breast and to be correctly lined if it is to house a wood-burning stove with its cement-attacking creosote condensation products. Make sure it is installed by someone who knows what he is doing.

If you were building a new house, any chimney would normally be expected to extend above the ridge. If your chimney does allow smoke back into your room, you should extend the stack to this height. Ensure that the top is rebuilt to its original design, or to a design that is usual for the area.

The top cap may be flat, sloping or pitched, and there may be one or two holes below it on each of the four sides. Often the top bricks are left unpainted, but in other areas it may be usual to render and paint these to match the rest of the stack Occasionally, we have seen stacks in which the top openings that face the ridge have been blanked off in an apparent attempt to defeat the down-draught which often results from the wind blowing straight over the ridge; we intend to try this method, but we have our doubts about its effectiveness. Revolving cowls are also available, and you may decide to fit one of these if the problem is severe, although the external appearance is rather unsightly. We have seen two different types; one constantly revolves with a turbine-like action, and the other rotates so that the outlet faces away from the wind. We would be interested to hear from any readers who have successfully fitted either type.

You shouldn't be too despondent if your first test firing results in an indoor smog. A cold, damp, new chimney never draws successfully and will always improve beyond all recognition on subsequent occasions. Smoking can also be greatly reduced by using firelighters and really dry starting wood, to get it going as quickly and cleanly as possible. However, it must be pointed out that chimney design is not as simple as it might appear, and it may be worth calling in an expert if you have continued problems and intend to make frequent use of your open fire.

CHAPTER 9

TURNING ON THE HEAT

Draught prevention. Central heating. Room heating by wood stoves, electricity. Air conditioning. Gas water heating. Connecting gas. Using solar energy.

Don't be misled into believing that stone fincas are cosy in winter, just because the walls are so thick. They're not. Stone may be a reasonably good insulator, but heat does leak slowly through it. Moreover, it needs a lot of heating before the walls no longer feel cold to the touch. In mountain areas, short periods of overnight ground frost are fairly common during the winter, and even snow is not unknown. Draughts are a constant problem and a poorly heated house can then be a most uncomfortable place in which to live.

When the wind from across the higher mountains, which are quite likely to be snow-capped between November and April, the temperature drops considerably and you are likely to feel the need for some form of heating during the evenings.

The original inhabitants of a finca are unlikely to have heated the entire room. Instead, they dressed warmly and huddled around the warm ashes set in a tray below a special round table called a *mesa camilla*, as we explained in the opening chapter. Nowadays we have come to expect room temperatures of at least 20 or 21 degrees Celsius, yet inside our stone-built finca in November (before we had properly draught-proofed it) we recorded 8 degrees, and a fan heater running all evening in a small room struggled to raise this to 13 degrees. If you are reading this while experiencing Spanish summer temperatures in the upper thirties you may find it rather hard to believe, but the fact remains if you aim to enjoy winter living in such a place you need to give some careful thought to the matter of room heating.

Draught prevention

Before wasting money on heating air that is immediately sucked outside with the inevitable draughts, it's worth investing in some efficient draught proofing. We were amazed at the difference which resulted. Hardware shops stock a good range of the usual self-adhesive foam rubber strip types, and these are ideal for attaching around doors and windows. At the bottom of the door I've found nothing better than the type that looks like a long brush embedded in aluminium strip. If these are not stocked at your local friendly hardware shop you can obtain them from one of the DIY hypermarkets to be found on the outskirts of some cities. Where there is a considerable gap beneath doors to the outside, it's worth unscrewing them from their hinges and glueing a strip of wood underneath. Even a home-sewn tube of fabric filled with sand, placed at the foot of the entrance door, can be very effective. Draught-proofing can also reduce or eliminate the constant howling noise which frequently upsets sleep in very exposed positions. Bear in mind that rooms do still need some ventilation, however, and this is especially important if you use gas for heating or cooking (where the ventilation will be checked before you can obtain your agreement for gas bottles), or if you have an open fire or woodstove.

Sources of heat

The main sources of heat in the campo are bottled gas, wood, electricity and heating oil, probably in that order of popularity. Each of these can be used for individual room heaters, central heating or (in the case of electricity) under-floor heating.

Bottled gas is the most popular because the delivery service is generally reliable in most areas, and it is reassuring to know that you have a reserve bottle standing by. We're not particular fans of portable gas room heaters, although the latest type have more efficient combustion and have virtually eliminated the usual odour. We always keep one handy for emergency use.

A proper fitted gas heater in a fireplace, or with a flue pipe to the outside, is a different matter altogether—efficient, reliable and free from smells and other unsociable habits. If, however, you are going to the trouble of having one of these properly installed, you might as well consider going a stage further and installing a central heating system, if conditions are suitable.

Central heating

Full central heating is usually run from the much larger and more economical size of gas bottles, stored in a locked steel cabinet on the outside of the house. However, before deciding to go ahead, make sure these can be delivered to your finca.

These large containers are difficult to handle and the gas company will probably insist on a certain standard of access—such as a concrete or tarmac track—from the road right up to your cylinder storage area. And the company imposes certain regulations, including specifying a 5 metre minimum distance between the storage area and the central heating boiler, the size and type of the storage cabinet and so on.

Wood stoves

Wood stoves and fires are fine in principle (and our preferred choice because they are so cosy and inviting), but they consume a surprisingly large amount of wood during a cold spell in the winter. Supplies of firewood (often gnarled old trunks) can be delivered to most areas and the local cost in 2003 was (all in cents per kilo):

Eucalyptus	12
Lemon	12
Almond	14
Olive	16

We were fortunate in having a large stack of slightly wormy, well-dried beams that came out of our old roof, and these have lasted us well. Cutting them down to size was a tiring chore, until Erna agreed—bless her—to bring my old electric chainsaw in her suitcase when flying out to join me. Never was there a stranger or more welcome item of baggage.

As a rough guide to running costs, a typical small stove will consume 2.2kg of dry logs per hour, giving off 7KW of heat. That works out at a cost of about 5 cents per KWH—slightly cheaper than electricity. However, you can reduce running costs by turning collected deadwood into heat!

Our primitive and quite large pot-bellied, Spanish stove consumed vast quantities of logs at great speed when first installed. We discovered that this was due to the rather loose fit of the ash box, which made it almost impossible to control the draught. We replaced the bottom metre of flue pipe with an equivalent length that incorporated a control flap, and the performance vastly improved—the heat going into the room instead of rushing up the flue. Its efficiency is now reasonable, but nothing like as good as the Scandinavian type we use at home. Note that pine should not be burned as it produces large quantities of tar (which soaks through chimney breasts, and which can also ignite) and of crystalline deposits which clog the flue pipe.

Flue pipes for wood stoves should be regarded as having a limited outdoor life. Ideally you should fit an insulated, twin-wall stainless-steel pipe, if you can get hold of any, but this is expensive. The stove-enamelled pipe seems to last longer than the thinner, galvanised type, but both types rapidly deteriorate at the point immediately after penetrating the outside wall, where condensation produces strong acids which eat into the metal. We have tried to prolong the life of ours by spraying galvanised pipe, inside and out, with heat-resistant stove paint, but we are not entirely convinced that this will prove totally effective.

All joints in the flue pipe should be well sealed, using a special heatproof sealer which is sold in cartridges to fit a standard gun. Follow the instructions carefully, allowing two days before applying gradual heat.

Electricity for heating

Both gas and wood have to be delivered to you along your track, so it makes good sense to stock up with reserves of both before the winter rains make access difficult or impossible. In theory electricity is a sound alternative in view of its high efficiency and ease of thermostatic control, but it is dearer than many other fuels. Also power cuts are not unknown in rural areas of Spain and the maximum power available to you could be limited by the overhead supply, often to 25 amps (equivalent to little more than two room heaters). Electricity is ideal for the many household gadgets and tools that run on nothing else, and for an emergency heater, but you should not decide to use it for major fixed appliances until you've sampled its reliability over several months, especially the winter months.

In conclusion, we recommend you always have a choice of heating using at least two different fuels, if not all three, to overcome any possible problems over reliability. Mountain winters in particular can be very chilly, and the time will come when you'll need as much heat as your various systems can jointly muster.

Room cooling

A finca may be chilly during the winter months but it can also become too warm for a comfortable night's sleep at the height of summer. That's when you will welcome the chance to relax in the refreshing coolness of an air-conditioner.

Air conditioners come in two basic types—basic, portable models (which normally have a flexible exhaust hose which can be led out through a window—less often seen nowadays), and those which incorporate a fixed wall unit. Both types can have an optional heating function for use during the winter.

The portable models have the advantage that they can be stored out of the way when not in use, but they are slightly less efficient as it is difficult to prevent some warmth creeping into the room around the outlet. They are also likely to be noisier, as the fan is within the room. The fitted type save on internal space, are slightly more efficient and are probably the better buy, but they need to be fitted by a professional. You will find many specialists advertising in the free English papers and magazines, who will be able to advise you on the best compromise between efficiency, power output, electricity consumption and noise.

Water heating

The obvious way of heating water would seem to be by electricity, possibly assisted by the free heat available from the sun. Electric water heaters are fully automatic, they can be turned on or off without worrying about pilot jets, and they are virtually maintenance-free. So why do so many finca owners end up using gas?

Well, often there's a limit to the amount of power you are allowed to take from the mains supply, and water heating takes up a lot of that allowance. Other appliances making heavy demands on electricity consumption include cookers, space heaters, jug kettles, hair dryers, instant showers and air conditioners, and if you have one or more of these you may have to reconsider your priorities.

Upgrading the supply cable from your nearest pylon, and the distribution board fuses, may not be the answer—the maximum power you can receive could be limited by the size of the cable between the pylons themselves. If your electricity bill says that you have a 20 amp supply, think carefully before going to the expense of running a new 60 amp cable up to your pylon. Apart from anything else, it could add to your standing charge if the supply company gets to hear about it. If you do draw more power than is available at any moment, up to the maximum allowed by your main fuse, what usually happens is that the voltage goes down below the official 220 volts. As a result, lights go dim and appliances work at slower speed or reduced output; if they were designed for 230/240 volts, the drop in performance is even more noticeable.

There is another drawback to electric water heating that sometimes tips the balance against it. The water throughout the south of Spain is very hard, which greatly reduces the life expectancy of the heating element. This wouldn't be such a bad thing if it could be readily replaced, but that's not always the case.

If you do decide to go for the convenience of electricity, check whether the element of that shiny, new white heater can be changed without major dismantling. Even if this is not the case, it may still be more cost-effective to regard the water heater as a disposable item every five or ten years, when compared to the higher costs of either fitting and maintaining an expensive water softener to overcome the scaling, or of buying, installing and maintaining a gas water heater instead.

Sink-top heaters

These little water heaters are useful mainly as an emergency or subsidiary supply, or maybe in a workshop or other single room that is too far away to be connected to the main water heating system. But as the average house needs hot water for the bathroom washbasins and shower as well as the kitchen sink, individual heaters are of limited use.

Gas water heaters

For many people, gas is the preferred source of water heating, It is dependable (as long as you have a spare bottle of gas in hand), reasonably priced, and relatively trouble-free.

Some larger firms of kitchen or bathroom fitters or plumbers may be able to supply and fit your heater, arrange for the inspection and the contract for gas bottles. Many people prefer to buy the gas heater themselves at a competitive price, arrange for a plumber to install it, and then request an inspection and contract from one of the gas suppliers (usually divisions of the same large companies whose names you will find on petrol filling stations).

Gas is an economical and reliable source of heat, which accounts for its popularity. A replacement for one of the Repsol orange *bombonas*, which provide us with about three weeks' hot water, costs (in 2003) just €8,12. New aluminium bottles now available from Cepsa are lighter and therefore easier to handle.

Whatever means of water heating you choose, you may be faced with the problem of fixing a heavy appliance high up on a wall built of stone and clay. Sometimes, against all the odds, you can strike lucky with normal heavy duty wall plugs and obtain a good, firm fixing. If not, it would be sensible to chop some deep holes in the wall and fill these with cement mortar, into which you later drill and attach your fixing by means of wall plugs or expanding bolts.

Always bear in mind that the weight of these appliances, when filled with water, can be quite considerable. If you have any doubts about your ability, ask the supplier to recommend someone who can fix it securely for you.

Try to avoid positioning a gas heater anywhere near a bedroom. If this is unavoidable, make sure any guests realise that there is always a slight "whoosh" and rumbling noise as the main burners come on each time a hot tap is opened. The only way to avoid disturbance at night would be to avoid using any hot water after the rest of the household has retired to bed.

If the finca is only used for holidays, it is a wise precaution when leaving to turn off the water mains at the meter (in case of any leaks from the supply into the property) and also at the main indoor stopcock (in case the other tap is tampered with). Any gas bottles should also be turned off at the regulator, with an attached label explaining how to reconnect the supply and ignite the pilot light.

Connecting the gas supply

If anything, gas should be treated with even greater care than electricity, which at least has the ability to detect and switch off if it detects any source of leakage. Nevertheless, the procedure for connecting a gas bottle to your new cooker or water heater is very straightforward, and within the abilities of a skilled DIY enthusiast, provided certain precautions are taken and the installation is carefully tested before use.

Each of the major gas distributors produces a helpful leaflet of *Medidas de Seguridad* listing safety rules and advice, and you should ask for a free copy before commencing your installation. It also explains what the inspector will be looking for, especially regarding the ventilation requirements which apply to all rooms where gas is stored or used. The gas cannot, incidentally, be stored in a basement or other room which is partly below the outside ground level. Following a satisfactory inspection, you take your certificate to the local supplier who will let you have your allocation of two bottles after a day or so.

A pressure regulator (el regulador) is attached to the top of the gas bottle (bombona), and this can be bought from many hardware shops; you will, however, normally be provided with one by the gas distributor, together with your two gas bottles, after the rest of the installation is inspected by them.

From this regulator is run a strictly limited length of a special orange-coloured 9mm plastic tubing. This is pressed firmly on to the regulator (wetting it makes the job easier) and attached by a screw clip. If the bottle is to be stood next to the appliance, with the shut-off tap of the regulator readily accessible and no source of heat in the way, the plastic tubing is probably all you need. The appliance is simply connected securely to the other end of the tubing.

If the path of the tube passes through a warm area (such as the back of a cooker), or if you wish to place the gas bottles some distance away from the appliance (possibly in another room), then a more sophisticated arrangement is needed. Between the end of the orange tubing and the appliance runs a special flexible copper pipe, 10mm in diameter, which is also available in a chrome-plated version. This pipe is very easily bent through gentle curves over your knee without need for any special tools. A nozzle is carefully soldered to the end of this pipe, to which the orange tubing is connected using a further clip. If the chrome plated type of pipe is being used, the plating must first be removed using emery cloth or a fine file, to allow the solder to adhere properly. In all cases use a good flux to ensure a quality joint, and avoid making a soldered joint too closely to a bend or you may find that the pipe is too distorted to allow this.

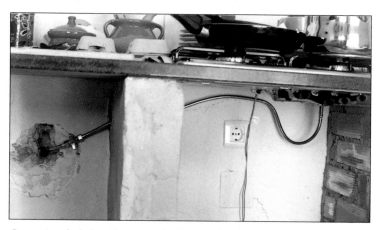

Connecting the hob to the gas supply (the oven has been removed to show this detail). The 10mm flexible copper pipe has an adaptor soldered to each end, one of which is screwed to the underneath of the hob and the other to the special gas tap. The tube is bent into gentle curves to pass through the oven supporting wall, and then out into the adjoining utility room where the gas bottles are stored.

This flexible pipe can be run through walls if necessary, after drilling a hole with a suitably sized masonry drill. Somewhere close to the appliance, and within easy reach during use, you then fit a gas tap. This will be supplied complete with removable flanged nozzles (which you solder on to the pipe), two securing nuts to attach the pipe to the tap, and - most importantly - a pair of washers which fit between each flange and the tap to provide a gas-tight seal. Finally the tap is connected to the appliance by a further length of flexible pipe, the exact means of attachment being explained in the instruction sheet for the appliance itself.

If you are able to borrow a friend's gas bottle and regulator, you will be able to pre-test the installation for yourself before asking the gas distributor to send along its inspector. Firstly, being ultra-cautious, we would suggest that you turn off the electricity at the main switch, and remove any potential sources of ignition. Switch off the appliance itself, as well as the tap you have installed. Double-check joints for tightness and then turn on the gas at the regulator. Wait for a minute or so and check that there is not even the slightest hint of a gas smell. If all is well, turn on the tap and check again. Finally, the appliance itself can be turned on and tried.

Should you have experienced even the slightest smell of gas at any point, which is extremely unlikely, we suggest that you abandon the exercise and ask a fitter to take over. The fault may well lie in the appliance or one of the fittings, and may require an expert to detect and rectify. Safety is all-important and must be your main consideration.

Solar heating

With all that free solar energy going to waste, it seems only logical to grab some of it to heat your water. Apart from the obvious saving in running costs, you'll be doing your bit to help the environment.

Solar heating is undoubtedly worthwhile if you live permanently in your finca, and the savings in fuel costs will repay the installation costs within a few years. If you use the finca only as a holiday home, the initial cost will be just as high but the savings will be less, so it may prove uneconomic.

Nevertheless, it still seemed to us very wrong to let all that energy go to waste, and an accidental experience finally spurred us into action. While waiting for our mains water supply to be connected, we had to fill half a dozen large green plastic containers each day from the village tap. We soon found that, if we left any of these containers out in the sun, they heated up very quickly indeed.

The first use for our lovely warm water was in an improvised outdoor shower, made out of a bucket, the tap from a water butt, and a watering-can rose spray. This was suspended on planks of wood between two walls at just above head height. Into that primitive arrangement we poured the contents of our sun-warmed container and we enjoyed luxurious showers at absolutely no cost, at a time when we had neither mains water nor any other form of heating. Painting the water containers in matt black paint increased their efficiency and - two years later - we continue to use them regularly in our outside sink, even though we have long since fitted a gas water heater.

With warm sunlight in such ample supply, it is easy to improvise a simple system that provides a modest quantity of warm water. This is an area in which it's fun to experiment, but in our case the development work was suspended once we discovered that—in our location—the mains water is quite warm enough for a shower straight from the cold tap during the summer months, as the supply pipe runs on or near the surface along several kilometres of baking hot track!

CHAPTER 10

WATER WORKS

The water mains supply. Connecting the pipework. Sediment and filtration. Water filters. Water softening. Regulating pressure. Shower fitments. The mysteries of the continental loo. Drains, and the pozo negro. Watering with grey waste and rainwater. Plumbing checklist. Knocking holes through thick walls.

Much of the straight forward plumbing can easily be undertaken by a competent DIY enthusiast, as it involves little more than soldering pipes together. However, the initial installation of the water heater will involve either a gas connection or some heavy electrical wiring, and you may decide that this is best left to the professional. Subsequent connections or extensions to this supply are much easier.

A plumber will also be able to advise you on the basic layout of your system, and this could avoid expensive mistakes later on. You might need to incorporate some form of water filtration or softening. There is a checklist at the end of this chapter covering these points. You might also need to incorporate a reservoir or depósito - and you'll find further advice on this in chapter 16 under "Battening down the Hatches".

The water mains

It's possible the agent who sells you the property without mains water does not know where the mains pipe runs. We were expecting it to be some considerable distance up the track, whereas in fact it ran right outside. The mains supply is rarely buried as deeply as it should be and might be exposed by erosion. You can often locate it by walking along the very edge of your *camino*, looking out for a plastic pipe (usually blue) where it surfaces.

This is the supply to which you will be connected after completing the necessary application. As this contract had to be approved and signed by the mayor in our case, a few weeks passed before the engineer turned up to connect us. Before signing such an agreement, check to ensure that you will be provided with a continuous supply, as some areas can only be supplied on a rota basis. This can be most frustrating, and makes the use of a *depósito* essential.

However, before the engineer comes you will need to ask your builder to construct the necessary access box beside the track. This has to be built to exact dimensions and so it's best to let him do the work for you. He can also liase with the *Ayuntamiento* on the final connection. The meter will then be installed and you will have the job of connecting, burying and taking into your finca the black plastic water supply pipe. If this passes beneath the track leading to your property, make sure it is buried at least a couple of feet below the surface to avoid any damage from passing trucks.

Knock a hole through your outer wall just below ground level (the technique is described later), so that the rising main will be conveniently located inside your kitchen or bathroom. Angle the hole upwards as it enters the house, and round off the top inside corner of the hole so that the pipe can more easily be bent into an upright position.

Our rising main of plastic pipe, stopcock, drain valve, pressure reducing valve, self-cleaning filter, by-pass loop and gauge. Where the system is going to be extended in future, for connection to a water deposit, a compression stop has been fitted; this can be readily exchanged for a straight compression union when needed, re-using the existing olive and clamp nut.

The pipe terminates in a special plastic compression adaptor, into which fits your main indoor stopcock and into that you can fit your 15mm copper pipe. These adaptors are very reliable, and if you do experience any leaks it is invariably due to reassembling the various components and seals in the wrong order - so make a careful note of how these go when you take it apart. Make sure that this copper pipe is firmly attached to the wall at two points above the stopcock to prevent any movement and subsequent risk of leakage

Connecting the pipework

The plumbing work itself is reasonably straightforward, being based upon standard sizes of pipe, screw fittings and joints. You won't find many brass compression fittings in Spain, nor pre-soldered unions, so you'll have to get used to the plain end-feed solder connectors. The secret of success with these is to clean inside each coupling, and the outside of each pipe end, very thoroughly with steel wool, followed by a smear of flux before joining the pipe. The pipe itself should be cut to length using an inexpensive pipe cutter. Not only does a hacksaw leave a jagged finish but the particles of copper it creates can fall into the pipe and damage appliances.

Before starting any soldering work, screw the pipe clips to the wall, using a spirit level or plumb line and pencil to ensure that the pipe run is perfectly straight and level (or upright). Minor changes in angle are best carried out using a pipe-bending spiral, but unless you can afford to buy or hire a proper pipe bender we would suggest that it is probably better to use soldered joints for your 90 degree bends.

When all of the pipes on a section of the plumbing have been cleaned, fluxed and pushed into place, apply the blowlamp to both the ends of the pipes and to the fittings until the latter start to discolour slightly, then run the end of the solder around the end of the pipe until it runs into the gap and you see a continuous bright ring of molten metal on the surface. Remove the heat and allow plenty of time for the joint to set before moving it. Finally, wipe off any surplus flux, particularly if it is the "active" type which can corrode the pipe in time.

Threaded connections should be made watertight by the use of PTFE tape, wound clockwise from the end of the thread, and you should use sufficient turns of tape (usually more than you think!) so that a slight resistance is felt when tightening the fitting. Tape is not required in fittings which are made watertight through the compression of a washer, such as when joining a flexible connector to a toilet cistern.

Spanish plumbers usually pressure-test their installations, but this is mainly because they sink so many pipes into concrete floors or walls where they would be very difficult to repair at a later date. We would be more concerned about long-term corrosion in such cases, and prefer to set them in accessible channels.

Where pipe work terminates in a threaded adaptor, the Spanish normally use a solder joint into the adaptor, where we would expect a compression fitting to be used. This is quite a tight fit (leaving little room for solder), and we always take particular care before soldering this to clean the joint thoroughly and apply plenty of flux. Such adaptors cannot be rotated for screwing into position after the joint has been soldered, so plan the sequence of your work carefully to allow for this, and add a rotating joint (such as a tap adaptor or a flexible connection) into the system when necessary.

There will also be times when you need to fit a short stub or "tail" to a joint or adaptor before attaching it to the rest of the system. You will notice two types of thread in use, often at the same time, these being the coarse $1/2$" BSP thread on the supply side and the finer 15mm metric for taps and cistern inlets. Most fittings and adaptors make it easier for you by having the size "$1/2$" or "15" moulded into them. You will probably find that you need to use several M$1/2$"/F15mm brass couplings in your installation. The $1/2$" thread is attached with plenty of PTFE tape while the 15mm fitting normally seats against a sealing washer.

Although you will use 15mm copper pipe for the majority of your plumbing, it is usual to supply bath taps from 22mm pipes to ensure a good flow. Many people never fit a bath and prefer to install an efficient shower instead, in which case no 22mm pipe will normally be needed in your installation.

The taps you buy in Spain may be an unfamiliar washer-less ceramic disc type but these can be very efficient. They are very light to operate and need no maintenance in normal use. If one ever starts to develop a slow drip, you can unscrew and replace the complete insert which is self-contained - the tap body plays no part in the seal.

Ask about any local water regulations relating to such things as isolation valves, non-return valves and the like, particularly regarding outside taps, and make sure your shower hose is not so long that the head can be immersed in the water of the shower tray.

Water filters

We made the initial mistake, in our anxiety to get connected, of running the main supply straight into the taps and toilet cistern. The latter became so choked with lime that it stopped working every couple of days. We noticed that particles collected in the conical flow-reducer inside the inlet valve, so we removed this completely and the problem was greatly reduced. However, blockages eventually built up elsewhere in the cistern, so a small filtration unit was the obvious answer. We fitted this vertically in such a way that the sediment dropped down into the main cold water feed pipe and was flushed harmlessly out through our aps, eliminating the need for constant replacement of the filter element.

If you fit a filter that has a transparent chamber, it is important to locate this away from sunlight, and to drain it completely when you are away for several weeks or more, to avoid the build-up of algae and bacteria. It should be installed with a by-pass loop and isolating valves. If you design and manipulate the valves correctly, you can arrange a reverse flow to flush out any sediment through a drain tap. It is unwise to choose a filter with a finer element than you need, as this will only block up more frequently.

50-100 microns is more than adequate. But check your water quality first, as you may find that no filter is needed.

Often it's possible to overcome a minor sediment problem by a simple redesign of the plumbing system within the finca, as shown in the diagram. When the supply to the kitchen taps runs horizontally, and appliances are fed by a vertical spur upwards from that pipe, small amounts of sediment can settle down to the level of the horizontal pipe when that appliance is turned off, and will then be flushed along the main pipe and out of the tap on the next occasion that this is used. Separate water filters can sometimes be fitted in a similar way (even if this means fixing them upside down), so that the sediment is carried away rather than accumulating within the unit. We adopted this approach when protecting the inlet valve of our toilet.

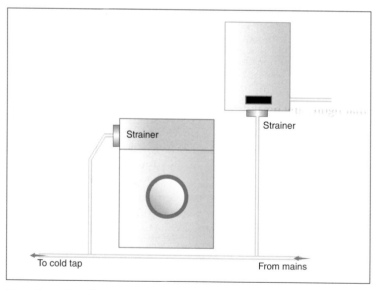

Strainer

Strainer

To cold tap

From mains

Many domestic appliances such as washing machines and water heaters incorporate a basic strainer filter in their inlet. If installed as above, small amounts of sediment in the mains water will settle in the low-level feed pipe and then be safely flushed out through the cold tap; this may eliminate the need for a separate filtration unit.

If you do not fit a filter, make sure you can readily access the removable filter which is provided at the end of the inlet hose of your washing machine, as you may need to remove this and flush it out at regular intervals. Remember that most washing machines sold in Spain have only a cold water feed.

High water pressure

You may also need to regulate the water pressure. This is because the mains supply to properties in a mountainous region has to reach a range of altitudes, and must be delivered at a pressure sufficient to reach the highest. If you are lower down, the water will reach you at a higher pressure. (Pressure is also likely to fluctuate, particularly if there is much building work nearer the source of the mains, or someone is filling a large water deposit.)

Pressure is measured in bar (multiples of barometric pressure), and most appliances are designed to work at a maximum pressure of below about 8 bar. Some domestic appliances—particularly those which incorporate valves such as washing machines, dishwashers, water heaters and toilet cisterns—can only operate properly within a limited pressure range. If your pressure exceeds that figure, any breakdown is unlikely to be covered by the manufacturer's guarantee, and a pressure reducing valve must be fitted.

These are not particularly expensive, costing around €20 plus a further €5 or so for a gauge. It is not always understood that simply turning down the main stopcock will not reduce the pressure, but only the rate of flow, and if you try to control pressure in this way you will always notice a sudden rush of water each time a tap is turned on. Incidentally, when we fitted our pressure-reducing valve, we also added a by-pass loop and valve, enabling us to test the unregulated pressure from time to time, and to take advantage of the extra pressure on those rare occasions when it may be needed.

If you are unsure whether you need a reducing valve, we would suggest fitting a pressure gauge in the first instance. This will give an accurate reading of the pressure, and it is also useful for its advance warning of a coming water shortage. If your pressure ever approaches 7 or 8 bar, we would strongly advise fitting a valve, which will have an adjuster which would enable you to reduce this to a comfortable level of 3.5 to 4 bar. However, you should not regulate the water pressure down to less than about 3 bar or the flow through a small-bore mixer tap might be insufficient to turn on a gas water heater.

With most rural water supplies, there are times when the mains pipe does nothing more than gurgle, and water frustratingly refuses to arrive. Usually this lasts for only a day or so (often, we find, on a Sunday when local part-time finca owners visit to irrigate their crops and top up their *depósito*). However, when the cut lasts for a week or more, as has been known, it can cause greater inconvenience.

Those are the times when we wish we had incorporated a *depósito* tank, acting as a reserve supply for non-drinking water. These can be built on site out of concrete blocks, or a ready-made plastic version can be bought. According to the location they may be emptied by gravity flow or via an electric pump. They can also be designed to incorporate a sediment trap, with a separate tap, and if well designed this could eliminate the need for a separate filtration unit—see page 191.

Water softening

Water throughout southern Spain is notoriously hard and the resulting scale can cause problems with heating elements, including those in kettles and washing machines. Water softening equipment is readily available but is extremely expensive and you will still need to by-pass the unit to provide a healthier unsoftened supply to your kitchen tap for drinking purposes (unless you use bottled water). There are, however, alternatives. You can try one of the myriad water conditioners that surround your mains pipe with magnets or electronically-produced impulses intended to keep the calcium salts in solution, if you are convinced that they really work.

Without such equipment, you will find that kettles need regular de-scaling (every few weeks in our case). We haven't come across any de-scaling solutions in Spain based on formic acid, but they often buy instead - rather alarmingly - bottles of 25% hydrochloric acid, as sold by many supermarkets and grocers. This needs to be well diluted before use, taking great care to protect your eyes and being sure to add the acid to the water rather than the reverse.

We were reluctant to use this at first, thinking that it would dissolve the metal of the element, but in fact it works very efficiently and the element looks as good as new. It is not, however, recommended for coffee machines, so you might still need to find a supply of the milder type.

As for washing machines, Calgon tablets are easily obtainable in Spain, and when used as a preventative will greatly extend the life of the heater element. Descaling tablets and liquids can also be used in washing machines and dishwashers, although the quantity needed is considerable and this is one of those cases where "prevention is better than cure".

Electric water heaters are usually more difficult to de-scale as the element is often difficult to reach or replace, and it is sometimes quicker to drain and remove the boiler for chemical de-scaling.

Showers

For us, it was a real breakthrough when we were able to enjoy hot outdoor showers at the turn of a tap, after connecting a shower head to our new hot water supply via a normal hosepipe, and the accompanying sea view was a bonus. With our gas water heater, we found that the perfect temperature can be reliably maintained by adjusting the control knob to a fairly low position. In this way, we managed without an indoor shower for over a year, at all seasons, until the five-star luxury of an inside shower cubicle was fitted.

When fitting the shower, you may find that you can only use a manual control valve if you have a normal "supply on demand" type gas water heater. This is because a thermostatic valve may reduce the flow of hot water in the summer to the point where the gas cuts out, resulting in sudden fluctuations of temperature and flow. If you have any doubts about this, you may consider employing a plumber to fit the shower valve, so that it becomes his responsibility to change it if this proves to be necessary.

The mysterious workings of the continental loo

Toilets in Spain - and throughout most of Continental Europe - may be different to those you are accustomed to elsewhere. Instead of the cistern emptying itself through a lever-operated syphonic action, a push button on top is used. And the mechanism that controls the level of water inside the cistern is a much lighter arrangement than the familiar ball valve.

When assembling a continental cistern mechanism, don't be too alarmed when you first peer into the bag and see the hundreds of tiny plastic components looking for all the world like an Airfix model kit. Assembly is quite straight forward, as most of the major units are pre-assembled for you, but do make sure you ask for an instruction sheet as these aren't always included in our experience. Instructions will be in Spanish but the diagrams are usually self-explanatory. A similar type of inlet valve is also used on the depósito.

Drainage: the pozo negro

The 100mm soil pipe from the toilet terminates in something which the Spanish builders call a *pozo negro*, meaning a black pit. I'd describe it as a leaky cesspit, each side being about eight bricks long and twelve bricks deep, with gaps in the side walls at regular intervals. Although primitive, it seems to be generally accepted as the norm, in remote areas at least. However, where there is more intensive development, the rules are being tightened and the fibreglass bottle-shaped type is often specified, so check local regulations first.

It's important to have a proper cover - a central concrete beam supporting one-metre long raciones, then a good layer of reinforced concrete on top, covered with soil and with a raised, lockable steel access door which gives a good airtight seal. (We can't imagine that such a thing could ever need emptying, but the facility must be there.) Make sure that there is no possibility of vehicles driving over the tank, as this would require the top to be constructed to an extremely strong (and more expensive) standard.

Successive stages in the construction of a pozo negro. Brick walls have been built, a cross-support fitted and raciones laid. On top of these the layer of reinforced concrete is about to be added.

Watering with grey waste

It is common practice in the campo for "grey waste" from the drain of a bath or shower to soak away among the olives and provide a degree of irrigation. This possibly unofficial system is something you can design for yourself, cutting holes or nicks in a piece of standard drain pipe buried just below ground level where it will hopefully increase the yield of your olive or almond trees. If you do a lot of cooking in your kitchen and the waste from the sink is likely to contain much greasy water, it might be better to direct this into the pozo negro, otherwise there would be a higher risk of undesirable odours developing.

When fitting waste pipe, you may encounter instances when it might need to be bend through an angle other than the standard 90 and 45 degrees. It is, however, quite a simple matter to bend a PVC waste pipe to any other angle you wish with the aid of a blowlamp. While wearing thick gloves and slowly rotating the pipe, play the flame along about a six-inch band for around a minute until it feels slightly rubbery. If you notice the first signs of scorching you have gone a little too far, but no harm will have been done. Then gently but firmly bend the pipe and hold it in place for a couple of minutes while it hardens (or, if you're impatient, douse it in cold water).

Using rainwater

If you have fitted guttering and have a means of storing the rainwater, make sure you put this to good use. Being softer than the mains supply it is excellent (if fresh) for rinsing hair, and - as it's free - it should be used for irrigating your plants before resorting to the metered supply. Underground tanks hold the greatest amount but you normally need a pump to extract it, whereas ordinary water butts have the advantage of being above-ground and therefore accessible by gravity feed.

Plumbing Checklist

Throughout your system, we would suggest that you simplify any future maintenance by fitting isolating valves on the supply pipe to each tap and appliance, and a drain cock at the lowest point on the system. Check through the following points before finally deciding on the design of your plumbing system:

* Is your water heavily sedimented with chalk or sand, which can block valves and showers? If so, you may need to incorporate a sediment trap or filtration unit.

* Is the water excessively hard? Most of Southern Spain suffers from this condition. A water softening (decalcification) unit may be worth considering, as this will extend the life of all types of water heater.

* Do you have a south or south-west facing roof? Do you intend to live permanently in the finca? If so, solar water heating could greatly reduce your water heating bill.

* Is the water supply totally reliable? If not, you may need a depósito to keep at least a day's supply in reserve.

* Is the water pressure constant and within normal limits - or does water sometimes emerge from the tap rather violently when you first open it? High pressure places greater demands on seals and valves, and an inexpensive, adjustable pressure regulating valve and gauge will save you money in the long term.

If any of the above may prove to be necessary, it's usually simpler and cheaper to incorporate them in your system from the outset.

Running pipes through thick walls

Walls can be up to 85cm or more in thickness, which presents something of a problem when it comes to extending the plumbing or wiring into an adjacent room, or running a waste pipe to the outside. First we start the hole with a long, thin cold chisel and club hammer, altering the path if necessary to avoid any impenetrable stones. Having reached the chisel's limit, we replace it with a metre-long piece of heavy concrete reinforcing rod or round window bar, hammering as before.

This technique usually results in a neat, clean hole. If you come across a complete barrier to further progress, you will either have to finish the job using a long masonry drill or start again somewhere else. If the hole is intended for pipe-work, try to keep it exactly horizontal so that your connections can run neatly in straight lines and right angles.

CHAPTER 11

MAKING THE SPARKS FLY

Mains supplies in the campo. Increasing available power. Room wiring layouts. Fixing the conduit. Lighting. Adaptors and plugs.

If there is no electricity supply to the finca and the supply line runs nearby, it is usually a relatively simple matter to apply for a connection, and an estimate can be obtained in advance. If the supply has to come from far away or if it needs stepping down from a high tension grid, not only will the cost be much higher but the delay is likely to be greater.

The main supply cable from your nearest pylon will normally run to a bracket on the wall which takes the strain, down the front wall, back upwards in a slight loop (to shed water), and then into the meter beside the front door and through into the distribution box behind. Here it goes through a 30millisecond RCD (residual current device) safety cut-out into the bank of MCB (miniature contact breaker) trip switches, each with its maximum current marked on the front.

Both the mains switch and the RCD will be marked with the maximum total power for which each is rated. The figure you obtain by adding up the individual MCBs may be slightly different. Yet either of these figures may be higher than the maximum current which is actually available to you.

Incidentally, if you already have a pylon on your property, but it is either too prominently placed or you would prefer to eliminate the unsightly thick overhead supply cable, it's worth enquiring about the extra cost of running an underground supply. However, the underground section still has to begin from a pylon. If the nearest pylon is on a neighbour's land, so that the underground cable would need to cross a strip of this land before reaching yours, his permission would have to be obtained.

Increasing your power

Your electricity account will show the maximum number of watts for which the original owner applied. This may be less than you imagine, because the standing charge can depend upon this figure, and it is just possible that more may be available to you. The local electrical installer will be able to tell you what this is, and he can also check the thickness of your existing input cable to determine how many amps or watts it will provide. It is sometimes possible to upgrade this by replacing the cable from the pylon with one of heavier duty, but there is a limit to the power available from the overhead cable and in any case this is obviously a job for the properly equipped professional.

The supply from the pylon does not usually incorporate an earth wire, so this is something you must provide—preferably

The ubiquitous electricity pylon may be an eyesore but it does have its (strictly non-approved) uses! Fortunately this one, right outside our sitting room window, has now been removed, after considerable delay and expense.

connected to a special earth rod of copper or galvanised iron, buried at least a foot into the ground outside. One thing you can easily do for yourself is to press the "test" button on the RCD safety trip, and check that it turns off the electricity. This test should be carried out on a regular basis, as this device can literally be a life-saver if you should ever inadvertently cut through the cable using a power tool, or if a wiring fault should develop.

The electricity supply in rural areas is generally not very well stabilised, and you might notice the lights dimming slightly when a powerful appliance is switched on. Some types of electronic equipment can be sensitive to this fluctuation, and this is one of the reasons why laptop (notebook) computers are so popular. Even if the power is cut entirely while you are working on an important document, the computer will continue to run under battery power and your data will be safe.

If you need to run sensitive equipment containing electronic components from the mains, you should protect this against so-called "spikes" with an anti-surge device. Nowadays, it is not only televisions, hi-fi and computer equipment that need protecting in this way, as electronic components are found in most equipment which includes an electronic timer, such as a washing machine. Unless protected in this way, they should always be unplugged overnight or whenever you are out.

Room wiring layouts

Europe, except for the UK, has continued to use individually fused circuits based on the original, somewhat dated, concept. Although this system has been improved over the years with better cable, flexible conduit and safer cut-outs, it still requires greater lengths of cable and is more time-consuming to install. With this continental system, in order to extend into a new room you cannot necessarily break into an existing ring and then extend it. Usually the safest way is to add a further miniature circuit breaker (MCB) to the distribution box and run the new circuit all the way back to that, using existing conduit and junction boxes whenever possible.

The wires themselves are normally contained within flexible plastic conduit tubing, which is sunk into the wall. The conduit follows a curved path to facilitate threading the wires through, and so it is difficult to guess where it goes after the room has been plastered and decorated - a potential hazard when drilling into the wall later on.

At every point where there is a connection, such as when branching off into a different circuit, you need a junction box. The wires themselves are individual insulated wires. When your electrician threads these through the conduit, they need to be very carefully organised or the result would be a real cat's cradle of a tangle. We are sure there is no need to remind you of the inherent dangers involved in electrical circuits, which is why the final connections should always be carried out by a qualified electrician.

Fixing the conduit

Although it's wise to employ an electrician for making the final connections, you can keep the cost down by fitting the conduit yourself. Cutting the conduit channels into the wall can be done with a hammer and bolster chisel (slow), angle grinder (incredibly dusty), or a heavy duty SDS rotary hammer drill and box chiselling attachment (expensive). None is ideal, because the system was designed to be incorporated into brick or blockwork walls just after they were built, when it's easy to attach the wiring before the walls are rendered and plastered over. Little wonder that some finca owners decide on surface wiring instead, which is more obtrusive but a great deal less trouble to install.

Because of the mess that is involved, it's best to start thinking of your wiring layout at a very early stage of your renovation. By designing the most direct routes, you may be able to reduce the amount of chiselling considerably, using each conduit for the largest possible number of circuits. Maybe you can even run some of the conduit under the floor, explained later.

Some electricians prefer to avoid installing the actual conduit, regarding this as building work, but they are usually happy to map out the circuit routes on your walls using lines made with a washable paint. If you decide to design the layout yourself, the principle is quite simple, as you'll see in the accompanying diagram of a single-room circuit.

The wires carrying the mains into the room will originate from the distribution box but can pass through shared conduit and a previous junction box. They will run to a junction box for the new room, from which radiate the light sockets, light switches and power points. The larger size of junction box can connect up to eight conduits, but if this becomes too complicated, a further junction box may be used. The power sockets can run in series within a room (i.e. in one or more single lines), as the electrician will be able to run extra supply wires through the boxes to avoid a potential overload situation.

High-consumption equipment such as cookers and water heaters will have their own circuit, although we noticed that the electrician connected our single oven into the kitchen power circuit via a power plug and socket (although this was of a heavier duty type with flat pins). Specify single sockets where they will suffice, as you may be charged twice as much for wiring a double! If you are uncertain about anything, ask the electrician to check your layout beforehand, to avoid unscheduled delays when he arrives to install out the wiring.

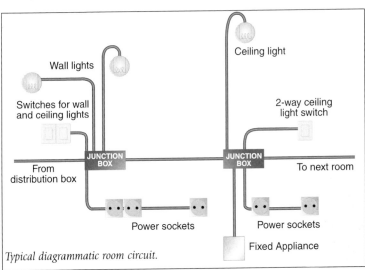

Typical diagrammatic room circuit.

Above: the wiring circuit was first roughly painted on the walls by the electrician. Bottom left: the tedious job of chasing out the channels for the flexible electrical conduit. Bottom right: conduit and boxes are fixed in place by patches of quick-setting yeso (plaster).

If you are employing a builder to do some or all of your structural work, it is worth asking him to cut the channels for the conduit and to engage an electrician for you. It might cost you a little more but you only have one person to blame if the whole system isn't fitted according to your instructions and fully operational. To make sure the power sockets and lights and switches are all fitted where you want them to be, you must supply the builder with a carefully marked plan, and keep a copy for yourself. Work to a colour scheme. Mark the power circuit in red and the lights in blue, for instance, with lines between lights and switches to indicate what links where.

It's best to indicate the exact height of light switches (normally at shoulder height, but the Spanish often fit them somewhat lower), as well as the height of power points and the number of sockets on each. Twin sockets are usual but you can have banks of three or four if necessary, which may be the case in a lounge (for the hi-fi bits), kitchen (for appliances) or study (for your computer and peripherals). Alternatively, a 4-way extension lead from a single socket will save you money if you only need to connect low-powered items.

While you're about it, consider whether you might need lighting and power in any garage, workshop or other outbuildings you may have. (See Chapter 3 for advice on preparing plans, as you might as well prepare a proper scale plan while you're about it.)

If you decide to do the channel cutting yourself using an angle grinder, be warned that this is a messy and somewhat hazardous job. Be prepared to invest in the necessary safety kit—goggles, gloves and a really good rubber dust mask with a separate filter canister. We have found that an inexpensive 115mm grinder is more suitable for this than a larger model, as it not only limits your cut to the correct depth but makes it easier to follow curves and get into tight corners.

Treat yourself to a diamond cutting disk, which could cost you as little as €4.50 from a superstore, as this will cut more readily, last much longer and create a great deal less dust. No matter what precautions are taken, the dust seems to get everywhere—even, in our case, into the next room after we believed we had taped up every small crack with masking tape—but at least we were in control of the situation and had only ourselves to blame for the mess.

The normal technique is to cut the two sides of the channel with the angle grinder, and then to chop out the centre using a one-inch wide cold chisel. The tubing used for the conduit was referred to as "macaroni" by our electrician but it's possible he was pulling our leg as the label on the reel described it as "corrugado". Sometimes 20mm diameter tubing is used, particularly for the lighting circuits, but our electrician preferred to use 25mm throughout.

If you are re-laying the floor tiles, as we did, you can save a great deal of chiselling work by running the conduit across the floor just below the tiles. To do this a slightly different, PVC-coated waterproof version of corrugado must be used instead. Where the floor conduit meets a wall at right angles, it then needs to run up the wall initially at a slight tangent to avoid a very sharp bend. It is quite permissible for some of the wiring to run on the surface of a wall, particularly in the case of lighting cable which is often clipped behind a beam. Where this is used, the normal three-core wire is used instead of separate insulated wires for the complete section back to the nearest junction box, including the part that runs in conduit before emerging on the surface.

If some of your walls are more recent and are built of hollow bricks, the cutting out is a simpler job. The sides can still be cut with the angle grinder to speed things up, but a flat bolster is equally suitable, and makes a lot less mess; then the middle of the hole is very easily chopped out to the back of the first hollow section within the brick. Thermal building blocks are also very easy to cut, being quite soft.

The conduit, together with the flush switch boxes and junction boxes, can be quite difficult to fix to the wall, and the junction boxes should be perfectly straight and square as - unlike some types of sockets and switches - there is no built-in adjustment. The secret is to press all of these into large blobs of the quick-setting Yeso YG plaster, about 60cm apart, which sets within a minute or so. Once the key points have been secured, the rest of the holes can be filled with cement mortar and finished with plaster in the usual way.

Most power sockets and light switches now incorporate an adjustable intermediate frame, which can correct a certain degree of inaccuracy in the levelling of the wall boxes. This does not apply to the covers of distribution boxes, which simply clip into place, so these boxes must be fixed perfectly straight.

Finally, take a photograph of each wall before it is decorated, rather than try to rely on your failing memory when you need to hang up a wall cupboard or shelf. Spanish wiring takes the most devious routes imaginable, and rarely follows the conventional vertical and horizontal paths that some of us are used to.

Lighting

If you use a little imagination when installing lighting, your rooms can really spring to life, emphasising the interesting texture of the rough walls and beams. There's nothing quite as dull as a single central ceiling light, although even this can be improved if you substitute an R63 type reflector in place of the original plain bulb. Better still, replace this boring arrangement with a couple of spot-lights, wall lights, up-lighters or even a standard lamp. Incidentally, most of the ceiling lamp holders on sale are only designed to cope with the heat from a 40-watt bulb and you will notice that few homes use 100 watt bulbs for room lighting.

Adaptors

Inexpensive adaptors are readily available in Spain to convert appliances fitted with square or other non-standard plugs, but try to get the type with thicker prongs which seem more durable, even though they still only have a rated capacity of 7.5 amps (=1,650 watts). If you want to use anything more powerful than this, such as a room heater or even an electric kettle, it is better to remove the original plug and replace it with a continental plug having a higher rating. Never try to fit a US plug into a Spanish socket as the

110v equipment will be overloaded by the 220v supply; transformer adaptors are available which step down the voltage, but they become increasingly expensive in higher-wattage versions.

CHAPTER 12

BACK TO THE FLOOR

Terracotta tiles. Laying ceramic floor tiles. Grouting. Sealing and polishing. Insulation. Repairs. Upstairs floors.

In Spain, where older buildings are concerned, flooring almost invariably means tiles. These can be of the chunky, soft, rustic terracotta variety, or - if a more modern appearance is required - you could use the thinner tiles of hard ceramic.

If you intend to employ someone to lay your new floor, it's important to choose the right professional. A general builder might make a fairly competent job of it, but a specialist will usually prove to be better.

However, there's no reason why you should not carry out the work yourself, particularly if terracotta tiles (losas de barro) are being used. These are readily available from virtually any Spanish builder's merchant. The most usual size measures 30x30cm, has a softer texture than quarry or ceramic tiles and costs the equivalent of only about 75 cents each.

The old floor can usually be lifted quite easily as it is normally laid on a fairly crumbly bed of damp sand-and-cement.

Many floors were replaced in the fifties and sixties in an attempt to modernise old fincas and have that sort of artificial ground-up speckled marble finish that always reminds us of a public convenience. Removing these tiles and replacing them with terracotta is the easiest way to restore rustic character to a room. Often they can be lifted quite easily, using a club hammer and chisel (we found a crowbar particularly useful), often taking with them the previous dry mix and leaving a firm concrete sub-floor behind.

Don't be surprised if you discover a disused well, or some sunken pots which were used to store wine, beneath your floor. One of our floors has a very hollow ring when tapped and we will be lifting this area with great caution. If you are fortunate enough to discover a well that can be brought back into use, there are laboratories in all major towns that will test water samples for quite a modest fee. This should be carried out at regular intervals if you intend to use the water for domestic purposes, rather than to irrigate your trees and crops.

Each of the types of tile mentioned requires a different technique, so we'll deal with them in turn:

Terracotta tiling

Terracotta tiles are fired at a much lower temperature than either ceramic or quarry tiles, making them softer and very much warmer to the touch. The most common and inexpensive Spanish version are relatively soft and brick-like. As they are so porous and contain air pockets, they have excellent insulating properties and feel quite warm to the feet in winter. The visual appearance of these tiles is also more mellow, but these tiles do need careful sealing and aftercare as they are very easily stained. They also benefit greatly from deep waxing to bring out their richness.

The floor is first concreted to within about 4cms of the finished floor level. To achieve an even, level finish you can use lengths of square section hollow steel for use as a *regla* (meaning rule or guide), which you can buy them from any steel stockist to be found in the industrial estates on the outskirts of most towns and large villages. They can also be used as lintels, and as supports for pergolas and for the the chains across the end of private tracks, so they are readily available. Buy as long a length as possible, but no longer than the width of the smallest room you wish to tile (even so, you'll probably need a roof-rack to get it home).

The height of these guides can be adjusted by packing out with slips of timber, but a useful product to use here is the quick-setting white plaster or yeso. This is also often used to set temporary uprights at each corner of a new wall when bricklaying.

Before fixing the tiles, lay some of them out on the floor with 15mm gaps between them. The first row should enter the room at right angles to the main doorway, and you should also lay out the back cross-row at exactly right angles to the first—again with exactly 15mm gaps. Make yourself a large set square out of a triangle of thin timber with sides measuring 3, 4 and 5 units respectively, as accuracy is essential. If it looks as if you will end up with very thin wafers of tile along any of the edges, adjust the start position to avoid this. Mark the positions of the edges on the bottom of each wall, and work to these marks—using a long straight-edge or *regla* —when laying the tiles.

The tiles, after being soaked in water for about an hour, are then laid on a bed of 1 part cement to 3 to 4 parts of medium sand—neither too sharp nor too soft. The top of this bed should be the height of the tiles below the finished level, the tiles normally being about 20cm thick. This bed should be rather drier than you would use for normal mortar—but not to the point of being crumbly. If you make your mixture too wet, the dampened tiles will sink into it and make it very difficult to lay a level floor, particularly if you use soft building sand rather than sharp sand. If it is too dry the tiles may be too loose and will rely entirely upon the grouting for their stability.

Tap down the tiles with a rubber hammer, checking the level and the squareness regularly as you lay them. One way to maintain that 15mm gap is to use offcuts of copper water pipe. As you proceed, you will be able to use a longer level - or stand your level on a long length of timber or steel - so that the overall level remains correct. When you reach the far end, work sideways and backwards, so that you end up back in the doorway and don't have to walk over the tiles you have just laid.

The terracotta tiles were laid in two stages, as the kitchen was in continuous use. On the far side the tiles have been laid and grouted (but not yet sealed). In the foreground the concrete base has been laid, into which have been set some lengths of the new electrical conduit.

Grouting

Wait 24 hours before grouting the tiles. You can then use either a fine sand-cement 4:1 mixture (which is perfectly suitable for 15mm gaps) or a special cement-based grouting compound that's better for fine joints. If you prefer a slightly darker colour, you can incorporate a small proportion of black powder additive in the mix, although this is rarely needed as the final waxing tends to darken the colour somewhat.

Try to avoid marking the surface of the tiles as you apply the grout by using a larger trowel to protect them, place a wedge of grout on this and then slide it into place using a smaller trowel. Chop downwards into the joint to soften the grout and eliminate air pockets, finish it off with a flat or rounded tool depending on the finish required, and finally wipe away any spillage from the surface with a damp cloth before it soaks in.

Sealing and polishing

As we have said, terracotta tiles are easily marked by fat or oil, and stained by wine and similar liquids, and this is a very real possibility in a kitchen. It is essential that they are carefully sealed and polished before the kitchen is used for cooking. Linseed oil is readily available from hardware stores and small supermarkets, but it should be the so-called "boiled" type, which in fact is not boiled at all but diluted with various solvents and additives to aid penetration and avoid leaving a sticky film on the surface. Ask for "Aceite de linaza con secante". Allow the freshly laid tiles at least three or four days (more if the weather is dull or damp) to dry thoroughly before oiling them.

Two coats will be needed, at 24 hour intervals, which should be applied after grouting, so that this is also sealed and protected. Any surplus which remains after ten minutes should be wiped off with a cloth. Then, after a further 24 hours, the tiles should finally be waxed and polished. Any good floor wax can be used, and the floor can be given an antique appearance by using a darker beeswax. The purpose of this final treatment is not to give a shiny appearance, but to continue the sealing process and bring out the full richness of their colour.

It is worth mentioning that some builders prefer seal the surface of the tiles with linseed oil before laying them, in a dry condition, on a wet bed of adhesive. Both techniques work, but laying damp tiles on a slightly crumbly bed gives better insulating properties and seems to be the more traditional method.

Tile repairs

If you are unlucky enough to break the corner off a terracotta tile after it is laid and firmly set, there is a simple way in which can carry out an invisible repair on the missing area. Coarsely crush a piece of spare tile with a hammer, mix with cement in the proportions of 3:1, and mix with a 30% PVA solution to form a thick paste. Wet the broken edges well and fill the missing area, leaving the top slightly proud; cover with plastic and allow to set slowly. When completely dry, grind down to the correct level by rubbing with another piece of tile.

Laying ceramic tiles

These should be glued into place on a really smooth, polished screed of cement and sharp sand using a special adhesive. It is essential for that screed to be perfectly flat, so you may prefer to entrust this part of the job to a skilled plasterer or builder, as it is difficult to achieve a perfect finish without previous practise.

If you want to tackle it yourself, we would suggest that you start off by laying as good a fine concrete floor as you possibly can, and then pour self-levelling screed on top. This protein-rich substance has the ability to level itself out and form a strong surface, even in very thin layers. However, it is quite expensive, and you may well find that it would have been cheaper to employ a skilled tradesman in the first place.

If the floor is already tiled, and is in good condition, there is no need to remove the original tiles. You can simply re-tile on top of the existing floor. The tile stockist will be able to supply a suitable adhesive for this purpose.

In either case. the adhesive is applied with a comb-shaped spreader which leaves a ridged finish in case the floor isn't perfectly flat. These tiles are laid closer together than the terracotta type, and X-shaped plastic spacers are available specifically for floor tiles, the usual thickness being 3mm or 4mm, to ensure a constant gap.

In areas likely to experience dampness, such as a bathroom or beneath a covered porch, a special waterproof adhesive must be used. In all cases it is important to follow the manufacturer's instructions. Then, usually 24 hours after the tiles have been laid, you fill the gaps with a fine grouting mix, rather than the normal sand/cement that is used in the thicker gaps between terracotta tiles.

One of the rooms in our finca was covered in old tiles of the traditional Moorish pattern often seen in Andalucía, which were well worth preserving even though a certain amount of patching and repairing was needed. Similar patterns are now being reproduced and can be found at specialist tile suppliers.

Upstairs floors

You'll find some advice on making the floor to provide an upstairs room at the end of chapter 8. If you already have such a room but the floor is deteriorating and becoming crumbly or chipped, you can often improve it by applying a thin slurry of neat cement mixed into dilute PVA (no sand is needed) and polishing this to a smooth finish using a steel float. In either case, you can tile the floor in the usual way, but we would suggest using the thinner ceramic tiles rather than terracotta, in order to keep the additional weight to a minimum.

CHAPTER 13

WORKING WITH WOOD

Making your own windows and doors. Fitting and hanging. Door furniture. Security and window bars. Kitchen units. Building brick pillars. Shelving.

Windows

Windows are important to the character of a building. Changing a window can alter the appearance of the building; make a bad mistake and you spoil the whole effect.

The original windows in most fincas are very small, and often there are no windows in the gable end walls that have no eaves to shade them from the sun. There is a very good reason for this - windows let in heat in summer and lose heat in winter. So think very carefully before you install vast modern windows and—worst of all—ugly patio doors.

Take a careful look at the original windows, because they can tell you a lot about the history of the building. In rooms which were used as animal quarters they will probably be unglazed and open to the elements apart from a few steel bars or a wooden shutter (which may be cut from a single piece of wood).

If the windows are beyond repair, with frames that have completely rotted at the corners, you will have to replace them. The usual way is to have replacements made locally. Most towns and large villages have their own joinery works and they will follow whatever plans you can provide - or match an original. In our case we supplied them with a photograph which we had taken in a rented finca, and they came up with an excellent match! Alternatively, you can make your own, as described later.

If you really must increase the size of any replacement windows, we suggest you keep this down to a reasonable limit. In our case, after drawing up scale elevation plans and comparing various sizes, we decided that the original 70cm wide by 50cm deep windows could go up to 100x70cm, and no more. Ask them to incorporate a means of attaching removable frames covered in fly-screen mesh, unless you wish to organise this yourself.

Making your own windows

Making windows is a fairly skilled job and, unless you have had previous woodworking experience, we would suggest leaving this to the local *carpinteria*. However, it's not an impossible job for the more experienced home builder to tackle. In our case we had the downstairs windows made by a local firm, but constructed the smaller upstairs windows ourselves. These were less noticeable, which put less pressure on us to produce a perfect job.

The windows open into the rooms, of course (as is usual on the continent), and their design needs careful thought if they are to remain weatherproof under exposed conditions. Window section timber may be difficult to locate in Spain. Unfortunately you cannot use sections designed for outward-opening windows in reverse, as these will provide no protection against the elements! Many joiners machine their own sections, which can be done quite easily. If you have a circular power saw and a steady hand, you can cut these sections out of standard sized timber such as 50x75mm in several passes, taking an existing window as a template and adjusting the depth and position of the cut as required. A router and a sawbench will make the job even easier. You'll need one set of pieces for the surrounding frame and another set (or two for an opening pair) for the actual lights.

You can make your own window sections by scaling this diagram up to size and cutting standard sized timber to these dimensions with a circular saw.

The technique is the same for the window frame or the lights. Cut as much timber as you think you'll need, plus a bit more in case of mistakes as it may be difficult to make an exact match later

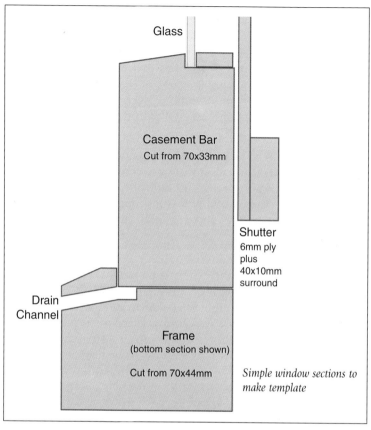

Glass

Casement Bar
Cut from 70x33mm

Shutter
6mm ply
plus
40x10mm
surround

Drain
Channel

Frame
(bottom section shown)

Cut from 70x44mm

Simple window sections to make template

on. Cut two pieces to the overall width of the frame, and two to the overall height. Make a line at each end, at right angles to the length of the piece of wood and the width of the wood from each end, as a guideline for your joints.

If you can make proper wedged, mortised joints, then you'll find it easy to make your own windows to match those being replaced. On smaller sizes, and particularly when making the frame, the less expert can use a simpler technique - maybe only a half-lap joint. If this is accurately cut, and held together with brass or stainless steel screws and waterproof glue, the strength will be perfectly adequate. Before screwing the four sections together, clamp them tightly in position and check that the diagonals are exactly equal.

You should also sight across the two lengths to make sure they are perfectly parallel. At this stage it's easy to make small adjustments by chiselling or filing the faces of the joints. The series of photographs illustrates the technique. Note how the screws are sunk below the surface and covered with dowels to give a more professional finish.

Wood needs to be treated against rot and worm in spite of the warm, dry climate. The walls it will be in contact with will retain a small but significant degree of moisture, from rising damp through the clay mortar, and at least one generous coat of a protective treatment before painting with the decorative finish is advisable.

You will also need shutters. If, like me, you are only making small upstairs windows, their shutters do not need to be a decorative feature and can consist of a piece of plywood, finished all around with a shallow moulding pinned and glued into place. Devise some means—say a long hook and eye—which enables the window to be held open for ventilation. It is also useful to incorporate a clip which enables the window to be held slightly open so that a small amount of air can be admitted throughout the night, even during the winter.

Finally, don't overlook the need for insect protection measures, by making some clip-on frames covered in plastic insect netting, so that you can fit these in the summer and enjoy fresh, cool air at night without being troubled by mosquitoes.

Doors

The main door of a finca gives it much of its character, but this is quite likely to need replacement when a finca reaches the point where it must be restored. An original door that is ravaged by woodworm and rot not only looks unsightly, but it will offer a minimal degree of security, and it is almost impossible to renovate without virtually remaking it.

Try and find a replacement that is as close as possible to the original design. If you cannot find one that is suitable, ask the local joinery workshop about the cost of having one made, taking a photograph of the original for them to follow.

You should be able to buy one with a simple, rustic design which also offers good security. The type consisting of vertical planks with visible bolts, rivets or studs, usually looks right, even if it might not be exactly the same as the original. The nail-on imitation studs may not add to the strength of the door, but they do improve its appearance and cover any exposed screws or nails.

Many fincas will have steel replacement doors, often fitted in the post-war years when timber was of unreliable quality. These are strong and normally very secure, but usually rather ugly. Try reducing the apparent size of the door by painting the outer frame white, and brighten up its appearance by over-painting the inevitable drab brown colour with something a little more pleasing - but nothing too out of keeping; the bright colours found in southern France, Italy and Greece are rarely seen in Spain.

Cladding them with hardwood panels might also be worth trying, and may at least enable you to live with the result for a few years until you can afford a complete new replacement. Other advantages of steel doors are the absence of warping, and the ease of attaching a security grille together with an opening glazed top half behind it.

Hardwood timber doors score every time for looks, but it is often difficult to weatherproof a timber door in Spain. Front doors usually open inwards, and so they cannot overlap at the outer edge and a slight gap has to left at the base for clearance; this cannot easily be sealed against the entry of water, especially if hot sun has caused the timber to warp.

Following a real downpour, you will see many local people at their front doors with their bucket and mop. Surprisingly, weatherboards are rarely fitted to the base of the door to deflect drips, though they can reduce the problem quite considerably. And always make sure that the rainwater running down the outside of the door has a direct path to the pavement or patio, by means of a drop in ground level or a slight slope to that row of floor tiles.

22mm thick tongued softwood floor-boards are available, from which you can make your own doors, cupboards, worktops and shelves. To cramp them together really tightly, we improvised this simple jig which comprises a pair of T-shapes, two further cross-pieces and two wedges (top). The door being fitted (left) has to be narrower than the original opening to avoid a ceiling beam. The door is supported in place while the gap is filled with bricks; frame brackets are built into the brickwork for a really firm grip.

Originally, fincas had few internal doors, and many Spanish families are still living in them with only the occasional door curtain between rooms. Nowadays we have come to expect greater privacy and fewer draughts. Doors are therefore needed but they should be in keeping with the rustic style.

If you need new doors, consider making them yourself. It cost us €420 to have a couple of softwood external doors made, but we subsequently found where we could have bought more than enough timber to make them for the equivalent of only €18 per door. From then on we made all our own interior doors to a simple shed gate design, buying tongued 22mm thick floorboard timber, adding the grooves ourselves, and then clamping it together across three cross bars using a system of wedges while the glue bonded them together.

Fitting the windows or doors

Fitting a replacement window or door frame is quite straightforward as - provided the frame is adequately treated - you don't normally need to fit a damp-proof membrane in an external wall. Make sure the frame is very carefully keyed into the surrounding stonework. Nails or screws are often used, with the heads protruding, but we prefer to use proper frame brackets. These are screwed to the frame and the prongs or serrated sections are cemented into the wall, after chopping out suitable over-sized holes for them.

If you are fitting a new or larger window which needs a new hole to be cut in the wall, you should first fit a lintel to carry the weight of the masonry above it. Old buildings had timber lintels, which were fine when new but less effective as they lost strength with age, weathering, worm or rot. If you were putting up a new building you would not be allowed to use a timber lintel. Even so, a treated timber lintel is more in keeping with an old building.

In cases where the lintel takes the weight of a high wall or upstairs floor joists, we would always play safe and fit a concrete or steel lintel, although a thinner section of timber could be let into the wall internally for decorative effect. Unless you have had previous experience of tricky situations like this, the fitting of a lintel in a load-bearing location is probably best entrusted to a builder.

Stone masonry is less predictable than brickwork and great care must be taken. But if there is only a small area of stone wall above the window, and no load-bearing structure above, it is often easier to remove the entire section of wall over a window and re-build it. And remember that small windows can be added immediately below a ring beam or structural timber without any need for a separate lintel.

Where we say "lintel" we include the plural of the word, for finca walls are so thick that it is usual for multiple lintels to be needed. These need not necessarily be at the same level, as you may need to stagger them so that you have adequate headroom above steps that are incorporated in a new doorway chopped out of a thick wall.

Door furniture

Internal doors in Spain are usually hung on open hinges, in which the socket section fitted to the door can be easily lifted off the pins attached to the frame. The alternative - which looks more in keeping with doors of very basic, rustic design - is to use black japanned gate hinges of the largest available size.

Gate hinges are normally associated with Suffolk latches and that is what we used, even though they are not usual in Spain. They give a very cottage-like impression but their drawback is that they cannot be very accurately adjusted to avoid rattling in a draught, although a small section of draught-proofing foam fitted out of sight can usually overcome this shortcoming. If you are a keen woodworker you may be able to carve your own timber latches, which would be more in keeping with the original style.

Doors that open to the outside have to offer a greater level of security, so they would be fitted with heavier hinges and - unless it is the final exit door - two of the heavy bolts on the inside into which padlocks can be attached. If the door opens inwards (as is usual) and is fitted in a thick section of wall, the strongest way of securing it is by means of a wrought iron bar which slides into recesses in the wall.

Security

Like them or not, security bars (*rejas*) are to be found everywhere, and form a useful deterrent against casual theft. They are also ornamental, and the finca somehow never looks finished until they are in place. Although we are not particularly fond of bars, we would not like to own the only house in the area that didn't have them. They are found on many of the oldest buildings and need not look out of keeping.

In fact, *rejas* are no modern addition designed to discourage burglary but are a truly original, traditional feature. Gerald Brenan, in his book "South from Granada", refers to these bars fitted to open windows playing a part in the courting rituals of the 18th Century. We can imagine that they could well have originated much earlier, probably to the times when windows had no glass, and that they were designed primarily to form a barrier against wild animals.

Even today, rejas are an essential part of the windows. In high summer, you're likely to have the windows open more frequently, and you may even remove them completely at times. That leaves an open access hole into your finca. Thieves are fortunately quite rare but campo dogs are not, and we once saw one dragging a whole mountain ham which it had undoubtedly snatched from someone's carelessly unsecured home. With bars protecting the place, you can leave the windows open (maybe with fly screens in place), loosely close the shutters for privacy, and leave the house without being quite so concerned.

Plain bars with no cross-pieces are fairly simple to fit. After measuring and marking the positions of your bars, which should be no more than 12cm apart (10cm if there is any risk of a child getting its head caught), you can start to fit them. Measure the height of the window opening, add 5 cm, and cut the steel bars to size. Now drill the holes for them.

Start by drilling holes of a slightly greater diameter, and about 5 cm deep, to take the top of each bar. You may need to funnel out the open end of the hole slightly. The bottom hole should be the same diameter as the bar and only 2.5 cm deep. Push each bar in turn up into the top hole, tap it backwards and let it drop into the bottom hole. Finally make good around any broken stones, and paint the bars with a primer and top coat.

However, a cross-piece does make the bars considerably stronger. If your bars have one or two cross-pieces, and are designed to be fitted within the window recess in the wall, you will need to fit these cross-pieces from the front by cutting grooves. Only one set of holes - say for the bottom - can be drilled, and the rest must be chopped out.

This is a less secure method and you should use a hard, strong cement when making good afterwards. Make sure the bars you choose are as unobtrusive as possible, while protecting your windows. Take a look at neighbouring properties to make sure yours won't appear too different.

Most towns have metal workshops that will make the grille to your design. Usually you'll find a blacksmith (*herrero*) or metal workshop (*la cerrajería*) among the factory units in the industrial zone on the edge of town, often close to the joinery works (la *carpintería*) and main builder's merchant.

Older windows often had the bars set into the frames themselves, rather than the walls, and this is another option to consider when you are having new windows made. However, don't assume that bars will fully protect your house against thieves and vandals. They won't. A good tug from a chain attached to a 4WD car will remove all but the most stubborn grille, and a car jack or hacksaw will quickly allow a slim intruder to squeeze inside.

If security is a problem in your area, talk to a security specialist about steel shutters and alarms, and make sure you are fully insured. Holiday home insurance is available in Spain through local brokers' offices, from one of the English-speaking insurers advertising in the expat press, or it can be arranged in your home country (possibly as an extension to your existing home insurance policy). Remember that an alarm is virtually useless if your finca is so remote that nobody would hear it ring, especially if you have no landline telephone which would allow a direct connection to the police or to an alarm company.

Kitchen units

If you are capable of making the windows and doors described earlier in this chapter, you will certainly want to build your own kitchen units.

The design of these is very much down to personal preference, but a very modern finish can look rather out of keeping with an ancient house. Timber surfaces usually look fine, as do tiles and cement, but plastics aren't ideal. Brick supporting pillars for the sink, or units of plain or stained timber can sometimes look better than polished hardwood, Melamine or Formica. Old-fashioned hanging curtains beneath the sink can be quite acceptable, and are easier to fit than hinged or sliding doors.

The first thing to choose is the sink, as this is something that must be plumbed in place and is a permanent fixture. Its position dictates the rest of the layout. We bought a traditional Spanish sink which is cast in white cement, complete with its pedestal base, but we decided that this was only really suitable for utility purposes and fitted it outside on the patio.

For the kitchen we were determined to have a "Butler" or "Belfast" type glazed ceramic sink, which seemed to us more appropriate than a stainless steel job. We were encouraged to see one illustrated in a glossy Spanish design magazine, but locating one was far from easy. The largest specialist kitchen supplier we could find said that they had received numerous enquiries following the article in question, but they could only suggest importing one from France. We knew from previous experience how long it can take to order things specially, and yet we did not want to waste more time tracking one down. We took the easy option and bought one in the UK, to be sent out by the removal company we use regularly.

The brick pillars which can be used to support kitchen units, sink, shelves and so on look really crude when first built (left), but when rendered (and later painted) they blend nicely with the rustic style of the room (right). Below is the finished result. The rendered support pillars have been painted, pine shelves inserted, and fitted with a granite worktop. We then fitted an integrated gas hob and electric oven.

This sink was supported on two short brick walls, which were rendered and painted white, and the sink was then plumbed in. This gave us the basic facility we needed to bring the kitchen into use. The rest of the kitchen was designed around the sink - fridge, work-top and draining board on one side, followed by more work surfaces and the cooker. Another brick wall supported the end of the worktop and shielded the units from the adjacent wood stove.

We originally planned to make the worktop from thick beech hardwood, but we were unable to track down anything that we considered suitable. The alternative was to make some shuttering and cast a reinforced concrete slab, which we would have tiled, but this proved impractical because of the cut-out around the Butler sink. We therefore had a granite top machined and polished to our specification, which was not exactly the cheapest option but it cost less than we had expected.

Most of the alcoves below were left open and fitted with pine shelves. Above the worktop was a single pine shelf, as we considered that wall units would have looked out of keeping. A painted solid pine food storage cupboard at the end, with a matching shelf above the worktop, completed the fixtures. The aim was simplicity and practicality, which we feel that we achieved quite successfully and at fairly reasonable cost.

Fixing to the wall

Fixing something securely into a stone wall, when putting up shelves or fitting kitchen units, can be a hit-and-miss process. The job is made a little easier if you use wooden brackets rather than the pre-drilled steel type, as you can re-drill them if necessary in a different place which provides a secure fixing into soft, firm rock rather than either clay or a really tough piece of stone. Best of all, fit two upright battens to the wall, and attach the shelves or units to these.

Heavy objects such as washbasins, water tanks or heaters are sometimes attached by the old-fashioned method using long rods or pipes hammered deep into the wall, but heavy duty expanding wall bolts can usually be used with success.

See: attaching gas heaters (chapter 9), and how to make a hole in a wall (Chapter 10).

Built-in shelving

The simple, traditional way to incorporate shelf units into a room is to build two narrow upright walls separated by a gap of just under one metre, fit flat one-metre *raciones* (roof under-tiles) as shelves, then render and paint the whole unit.

Other furniture

Much of the wooden units you see in showrooms, or displayed in the catalogues of village shops (where, incidentally, the prices can also be quite competitive), is also available at lower cost, on request, as unpainted white-wood. Ask for "en blanco, sin pintar". Even if you want to end up with a standard finish, you can often achieve a better result by staining and varnishing in clear satin (*satinado incoloro*) yourself in separate stages, rather than using the unattractive and easily scratched combined stain/varnish which is usually sprayed on at the factory.

One rather surprising way of acquiring further items of furniture is from the place beside a local minor road where several dustbins are kept for public use. It has become quite usual for household items which are surplus to requirements, or which require small repairs for which the owner lacks the necessary tools or skills, to be placed beside the bins in case they are of use to others. We have disposed of several items in this way which were bought with the finca but not required, and - we are not in the least ashamed to admit - we have also acquired a few which needed minor attention. At this moment we are restoring quite a nice upholstered stool which we came upon in this way, and we have welcomed the opportunity of using the skills which were learned at a long-past evening class back home. On a more organised scale, regular weekend flea markets are held on the outskirts of Fuengirola and Nerja, and there are numerous small salvage yards tucked away which sell things like old doors, fireplaces and furniture.

CHAPTER 14

THE SPACE OUTSIDE

How much land? What crops will grow on it? Drought resistant plants. Establishing and irrigating plants. Weeds and the fire risk. The patio: paving, walling, rainwater drainage, lighting. Creating shelter and shade. Built-in outdoor grills, sinks, showers, seating. Pools, Jacuzzis.

How much land?

The amount of land being sold with your finca will be quoted in thousands of square metres. In case these are difficult to relate to imperial measurements of area, just remember that 10,000 square metres are equivalent to one hectare, which is 2.471 acres. Therefore every 4046.8 square metres you buy equals one acre.

If the land is not already registered together with the house but is being sub-divided from a larger farm or estate, you should expect it to be professionally surveyed and the boundaries clearly marked on the ground by the usual white-painted rocks. This work will normally be arranged by your property agent, and a plan supplied which carries the name and registration number of the *ingeniero technico agricola* together with the official stamp of the *Colegio* with which he is registered.

After this is done, the land must be properly registered along with the house. Occasionally there are local circumstances which dictate that this has to be done as a separate procedure after obtaining permission from the Town Hall. Complications of this nature can involve you in extra delay and expense, and you should seek the advice of someone who is well acquainted with current legislation and with local attitudes to such situations.

Large areas of land are an added responsibility and can even become a distinct liability at times. Weeds have to be kept under control to prevent a fire hazard, putting at risk the property of yourself and of others, and if you allow crops to run to waste this could tarnish your local image.

The more fertile the land, the greater the potential problem. Our 3,000 square metres of rocky mountainside are easily managed with the minimum of work. After many decades of carefully tending our cultivated plants in a fertile English garden, it has come as an unexpected pleasure to watch nature producing a far superior display, without any help, on a rugged Andalusian hillside.

On the other hand, if you intend to live permanently in Spain and are really interested in growing things, a larger area of fertile land - particularly if it contains some mature and productive trees - can be a real asset.

Which crops will grow?

There's a lot to be said in favour of leaving the surroundings in their natural state, so that the countryside extends right up to your door. But it's part of human nature to want to create a garden and to grow flowers, fruit and vegetables. A sensible approach might be to set aside areas for cultivation - maybe a rockery or flower border to the front, a vegetable patch at the back - without spoiling the setting altogether.

So exactly what will grow around your finca? The answer will vary according to the aspect, altitude, prevailing wind direction, shelter, rainfall and latitude of your finca. But you can get a good general idea by taking a walk and noting the plants and trees that flourish in your area.

Undoubtedly, more plants are killed by drought than by anything else. If a plant dies for this reason, it means that the roots are collecting less moisture than is being evaporated from the leaves. This, in turn, can simply mean that the root structure is insufficiently well developed and has not yet penetrated to the deeper levels where a trace of moisture remains throughout the summer. Newly planted species of trees and plants that are virtually drought-resistant when full grown will still need regular watering throughout their first season, while the roots are still growing down into the soil.

Those olives you wish to preserve should be picked in late autumn while still green or just after turning black, leaving the rest of the crop to ripen fully for the oil harvest which usually begins around mid-December. Exact dates will vary according to latitude and altitude.

Foremost among the trees that can eventually survive with virtually no irrigation are the olives, of which a specialist nursery may stock several of the 30 or so varieties in cultivation. They can live to a great age, although they are often replaced when the original trunk starts to become hollow.

Almonds are almost as tough, although both will produce only limited crops following a prolonged drought. Figs, vines and citrus fruit trees are likely to grow with a small amount of shelter from the winds but they are dependent on a degree of irrigation during the hottest months if a crop is to be expected. Prickly pears will grow anywhere, seemingly without any water at all. Their fruit might have little or no commercial value, but we love it - and we will describe later how to pick this inconveniently packaged but outstandingly delicious crop.

Our four original almond trees produce a reliable crop and these are in demand as an accompaniment to the evening glass of fino as well as in cake making.

Various coniferous plants such as cypresses are widely grown, and form very effective wind-breaks. Choose from the selection offered by your nearest nursery, as these are most likely to be suited to local conditions.

The strawberry tree (Arbutus unedo) is an unusual and attractive large tree with edible fruits. It will usually survive without irrigation, once established.

Trees for ornamental purposes (as opposed to cropping) that usually succeed include various varieties of oak, including the Holm Oak and Cork Oak, and numerous evergreens including types of cypress and juniper. There is one common type of wild oak which has holly-like evergreen leaves little larger than a fingernail, which is as tough as old boots. It seems able to grow in the most rocky, exposed locations and to resist any amount of drought. It also grows very readily from acorns, and young saplings are easily found. We have seen these trees planted as a shelter hedge, only about a metre apart, and we are trying the same idea ourselves.

Drought-resistant plants

Among smaller plants, most herbs are of Mediterranean origin and will survive with the minimum of watering. Rosemary (*Romero*) and thyme are particularly suitable (the former is said to grow better if it has a view of the sea!). Most vegetables need regular watering if they are to survive the summer heat, although they can be sown in October/November or early February to give them a better start. Globe artichokes are supposed to be fairly drought-resistant, but ours failed. Surprisingly, perpetual spinach beet has proved more reliable, and seemingly lifeless specimens usually sprout fresh leaves after the first real rains of autumn. Potatoes are worth trying, as they also produce fresh growth in autumn and should yield a few new potatoes quite early in the spring.

Among flowers, geraniums (pelargoniums) soon grow into large, attractive bushes, and even the traditional English roses are popular in Spanish gardens, although these will need at least weekly watering throughout the summer period. Don't be too excited at the prospect of bougainvillaea covering your pergola with its exotic blooms, as this plant prefers a sheltered spot and rarely thrives in exposed mountain locations. More suitable climbers are available, such as summer jasmine.

Here is a list of plants which can be grown from seed, and which are most likely to succeed in hot, dry locations. Several of them are fairly recent introductions from South Africa:

Anacyclus	Mount Atlas Daisy
Acaena	New Zealand Burr
Alyssum Saxatile	Perennial alyssum/rock cress
Antennaria dioica	Cat's Ear
Arabis	Rock Cress
Armeria	Sea Thrift
Asperula liliaciflora caespitosa	
Cytisus decumbens	Broom
Dryas octopetala	Mountain Aven
Frankenia laevis	Sea Heath
Genista pilosa/pulchella	Prostrate brooms
Lavandula	Lavender family
Saxifraga	a large family of rock plants
Sedum	(but avoiding the larger sedum acre or album)
Sempervivum	House leek
Thymus	Various forms of thyme, most of them with culinary uses.

Aloe vera seems to be totally drought-proof in places where nothing else will grow, and it is also useful as its juice is said to be one of the best remedies for sunburn and other types of burn. Various related wild succulents are equally tough and offshoots can often be collected and planted. Bulbs are also fairly reliable, as they die back after flowering and spend the dry summer safely under ground. All the various ornamental thistles and teasels are also drought-resistant, and many of the really deep-rooted plants like comfrey can often manage to tap into a supply of moisture.

Establishing a plant

Most plants and trees sold in Spain are now grown in containers, and this extends the planting season considerably. You should have no difficulty in finding a suitable nursery or garden centre beside any main road in a predominantly agricultural area. Look for one where the plants are grown outside rather than under green plastic netting, as they are more likely to be hardened off and more readily established in their new location.

While most varieties can be planted at any time between November and April. In really exposed mountain sites, March/April is sometimes preferred, as this avoids too much loosening of the roots from the worst of the winter gales, but you must then water right through the summer to ensure that the roots become well established. If you decide to plant them in the autumn or winter, it may be necessary to protect them from cold winds with plastic tree shelters or by a circle of protective fencing during the first few months, to give them a much better start.

Until any tree or other plant can look after itself under hot, dry conditions it must develop a healthy, well-distributed root structure. The usual method of doing this in Spain is to dig a hole, somewhat larger than the root-ball, and then fill this right to the brim with water daily for a week or two. In rocky soil this will involve using a pick-axe or crowbar, followed by a mattock. If the going is really hard, dig a small hole first and fill this with water to soften the deeper soil and rock. Planting then takes place in this well-watered hole, surrounding it with a planting mixture consisting of the topsoil from the hole to which is added an equal quantity of well-rotted manure or potting compost. Consolidate the soil and water in really well.

Mulching is very important, as it is essential to conserve what little moisture there is in the soil. You can use black plastic sheeting, flat stones, shingle or - if you are in an almond-growing area - you can put those heaps of discarded, blackened almond husks to good use by spreading a thick layer around each newly planted tree.

We have noticed that spare almond saplings spring up readily beside the parent plants and appear to bear just as readily, so you may care to try transplanting a few of these in mid-winter, thus increasing your stock at no cost.

Irrigation systems

If you intend to establish new trees or shrubs while you are away, or cultivate crops which rely on regular watering, and if you are unable to find anyone willing to care for them in your absence, you will need to install some sort of irrigation system. Many of the latest type are connected directly to the mains, and operate on a minimum pressure of 1 bar; the water is supplied, sometimes via an electronic control timer, to a series of small drip-feed nozzles connected to small-bore plastic tubing. This system is fine when all goes well, but there is always some degree of risk in needing to have your mains permanently connected and turned on: any leakage due to accidental damage or vandalism can result in a hefty water meter charge if it goes undetected for any length of time.

We have therefore been planning an alternative system in which a simple irrigation supply comes from a high-level *depósito*. Whenever we leave the finca for any length of time, the mains will be turned off and the reserve in the tank will be used to drip-feed our most vulnerable plants. That will offer the added benefit of draining much of our stale reserve supply away, so that it can be replenished with fresh water upon our return. Naturally, the rate of flow will have to be carefully adjusted so that the tank lasts for the duration of our absence, but we are hoping that it will be better than nothing - and certainly less worrying.

In an emergency, you can set up an empty oil barrel beside a newly planted tree, fill it with water and drill a small hole (perhaps only about 1mm diameter) at the bottom. Such drums can often be collected, free of charge, from local builders' merchants, agricultural merchants or other small industrial concerns; obviously you will need to check that their previous contents were not harmful, and rinse them out well before use. This supply may only last for a few weeks but it could just be sufficient to save the tree from perishing.

The surrounding land may look attractive as nature intended, but you can still put some of it to good without spoiling the effect by growing productive crops.

Caring for your trees and crops

If your land includes some olive or almond trees, these will need regular attention to keep the ground clear, fertilising or manuring, spraying if you consider this necessary, harvesting and pruning.

It can be difficult to judge exactly when is the "right" time to do these various jobs, so watch what the locals do. If they are pruning their almonds, you should be pruning yours. Notice how many main branches they leave, what they do with the prunings, and be prepared to learn from them. You will also gain their respect if they see that you are caring for trees that may originally have been part of their own land.

If you have no use for a crop of, say, olives (bearing in mind that the processing factories will rarely accept small quantities nowadays), it would not only be wasteful to leave it on the tree, but it will reflect unfavourably on your general attitude. Let your neighbour pick the crop, and you may even find a bottle or two of olive oil on your doorstep in return.

Weeds

In the heat of a Spanish summer, fuelled by tinder-dry under-growth and fanned by strong winds, fires are a frequent risk and can be potentially very dangerous. Everyone who owns land has a moral responsibility to keep it reasonably free from heavy spring weed growth that can become a real fire hazard within a few months. How you do this is up to you. Various options are: scything or strimming the land around the beginning of May; asking a neighbouring farmer to look after the land for you, paid for either in cash or in exchange for your crops; or - as a final option only, and not personally recommended - spraying the land early in the new year to prevent the growth, even though this will mean denying yourself of the wonderful display of wild flowers that is such a feature of the Spanish campo.

Rank growth of weeds, as opposed to a balanced display of more modest wild flowers, often arises because land is too heavily fertilised, particularly with nitrogen. If you decide to fertilise or manure your trees, you must accept that this will also encourage weed growth, which may call for some limited herbicide spraying around the trunks. Any plant that is so dominant that it excludes all other growth is to be discouraged, or you will lose the diversity of flowers that makes the springtime so attractive. We had a vigorous form of wild mallow which - while attractive enough when in flower - allowed no other flowers to grow in its vicinity, and became a dry, brittle fire hazard soon after flower-ing. Cutting this vigorous growth hard back in early spring, using a small hand sickle, seems to be keeping it more or less under control, but we would be prepared to apply a non-persistent weed-killer to these areas if necessary.

Prickly pears have a habit of extending their boundaries—especially downhill—and will need frequent trimming to keep them in check.

During a prolonged drought, with little or no rain for six or seven months, even the prickly pears can suffer and the crop will fail—but the plants usually recover when the rains return.

Another weed that comes under the definition of "a plant growing in the wrong place" occurs when a useful clump of prickly pear decides to extend its boundaries, usually downhill. Left unchecked, prickly pear could eventually take over your entire plot of land, and it is claimed that an acre of these plants can weigh 800 tonnes - so clearing a sizeable area of these can involve some very heavy work. We like to maintain a strict patrol around the edges of the clump each year. My most useful weapon is a parrot-shaped pruning saw fitted securely on the end of a long pole. This is the only thing we have found which will slice easily through the stems and leaves. The old, woody "trunks" are even harder to cut and we have resorted to using a chain saw on these, although we find that the sprocket wheel becomes hopelessly clogged with pulp and needs to be cleaned out every few minutes. Chopping back is only part of the job. If you leave the prunings where they fall, you will end up with a much worse problem than before, as each scrap will root and grow. Scrupulous clearing up is essential, and the prunings may need to be dried before they can be burned.

The Patio

It's well worth allocating time and money on making a practical, attractive patio area outside the finca, as you can expect to spend a great deal of your time there. In fact, if you shade it from the blazing heat, shelter it from prevailing winds, add a seating area, grill and sink, you'll probably find yourself using it more than any inside room.

Before concreting the patio, we decided to build up some simple formwork to provide the necessary bi-directional slope that will ensure effective drainage (left). The whole area was then concreted, leaving holes in which the pressure-treated rustic timber supports for the pergola were later anchored. The patio has now been finished (right) in the same terracotta tiles that we have used on the kitchen floor.

The patio is normally located for convenience outside your front door, but you can build it anywhere where it is sheltered and private and has a good view. It is easy to make the common mistake of allocating too small an area to the patio. It should be similar in size to any other room, say 3.5 by 4.5 metres or a little more.

The area is normally defined by an outer wall, which serves to deter inquisitive roaming dogs and may also provide some useful seating. You can either construct this wall from natural stone or you can use bricks, in which case it should be two bricks wide, bonded together with frequent lengthwise "headers", then rendered and painted to match the house.

Its floor can be concreted (fairly practical but rather ugly), cobbled (uneven and eventually weedy), paved or tiled. We have decided to use the same terracotta tiles that we laid indoors (see chapter 12) as these are practical, attractive and inexpensive - even more so if bought by the pallet load of 144 tiles.

Rather than lay them in the conventional way on a compacted sand bed using a dry sand/cement mix, we first concreted the surface to a depth of 5cms. This proved very effective in combating the main nuisance problem of patios, namely the ants (particularly those tiny ones which get everywhere and can give an irritating nip). The tiles will then be laid using the same technique as indoors.

It's very important to incorporate an adequate slope for drainage, particularly if the outer walls create a barrier that could produce a pool of water. Aim for a minimum slope of 1 in 50, which in our case was conveniently indicated when the bubble of the spirit level was against the outer line of the marked area instead of being centred.

The slope should be away from the door and walls, and out towards the garden—or you can arrange for drainage holes in the side walls. The final level against the main doorway will need to be 1cm or more below that of the inside floor, to avoid heavy rainfall from creeping inside, so excavate sufficient earth to allow for this.

If the overall size is more than about 3m in any direction, it's wise to incorporate an expansion joint in the concrete. This need be no more than a piece of 25mm x 50mm timber which is used when setting out the levels but which—unlike any other formwork —is left in place and tiled over after the job is completed, and which will help to avoid cracking.

Pay particular attention to the edges of the patio, as this is where ants can continue to gain access. Keep some strong sand/cement mortar mix to hand during construction which can be trowelled into any small gaps.

Pergola and Shading

If you intend to erect supports for bamboo shading, and if this will be shorter than the length of the patio, you may like to incorporate some suitable holes in the base into which the uprights can be firmly anchored at a later stage. In our case, we set water-filled plastic mineral water bottles temporarily into the concrete at the appropriate positions, which were 1.9m out from the front of the finca. This allowed for an eventual sloping roof to be covered in 2m wide bamboo.

The uprights are available from wood-yards, such as the ones mentioned in chapter 8. They must be firmly attached, rather than knocked together with a few 75mm nails. We will be using a combination of coach bolts and galvanised strapping to resist the winter gales. We have still not decided whether to leave the bamboo roofing in place throughout the winter or not - it can certainly provide welcome shelter, but it remains to be seen whether it will survive the worst of the storms.

Protection from the wind

The wind is a talking point throughout the south of Spain, some places being more sheltered than others just a few hundred metres away. You can reduce its effect considerably on your patio by suitable screening, but this must be really well supported. Steel supports are strongest but timber looks better; we favour a sensible combination of treated and stained timber post uprights, with a load-bearing box-section steel bolted across the top of them, and then intermediate rafters of either material.

Before fixing your posts, we suggest that you carry out a simple experiment to determine the direction of the wind, using a strip cut from a thin plastic carrier bag attached to a stick. In our case, although the strongest winds come from the north-west, they eddy around the roof and walls in such a way that the "nuisance" wind actually blows back over the patio from the south. Screening is extremely effective as the filtering effect means that such eddies are reduced or eliminated. However, it's often difficult to predict just where it should be placed to achieve the optimum result, so be prepared to experiment before making your final fixings.

Useful side protection can be provided with thicker woven rolls - we can't quite work out from what substance they are made, but it's rather heather-like in texture - which are readily available and more effective than a completely solid barrier. Climbing plants can also offer shelter against wind, but don't expect the more exotic species like bougainvillaea to be happy under mountain-top conditions. We would suggest instead one of the ten or more species of summer jasmines, or better still take the advice of your nearest plant nursery. There are a few tough climbers which survive by nature of their pencil-thick, invasive roots that can force their way into your walls and do untold damage, so be careful to avoid these. We had to demolish a patio wall in order to eradicate one such plant from the front of our finca.

It's worth fitting an outside light above your front door to illuminate the patio, but it is certainly not necessary to use a high-wattage security light. Not only is this overkill and totally unnecessary, it will add to the increasing problem of light pollution. One of the great attractions of the Spanish mountains is the amazingly clear night sky in which you can see the most distant of galaxies. We have fitted a 60-watt lantern light which is used only when necessary. We find this perfectly adequate, and entirely appropriate for such a location.

The outdoor grill

While you are designing your patio area, consider incorporating an outside grill. Cooking indoors during the summer is not something I'd recommend, the heat produced making the kitchen far too hot for comfort. Besides, it´s much more pleasant to be outdoors.

We suggest that you design your own according to the situation and size you need. You can build it mainly of bricks or you can use local stone. The coals rest on a steel sheet cut to size at the local metal workshop, or on a grid of closely spaced rods or a sheet of expanded mesh if a better draught is needed.

Alternatively you may be able to buy an outdoor grill kit from a hardware shop or garden centre that includes the shelves for both the coals and the food. These are normally set two courses of bricks apart, and when in use this distance is almost halved by the depth of the charcoal bed.

The brickwork can extend upwards into a low chimney, as this makes the fire easier to light and control, and keeps the smoke out of everyone's eyes. We would suggest using solid bricks to avoid the need for rendering the surface to hide the ugly holes of the most common type, especially as the cement is likely to crack off under the heat.

Pools and Jacuzzis

Whether or not a swimming pool is appropriate to your location is for you to decide. Situated on a mountaintop exposed to public view, it seemed to be out of the question for us. But if we were in a more secluded place, with some flat ground nearby, we would certainly consider having one installed. What we do have is a small walled courtyard, and this seems to be the very place for something a little smaller in which to cool off - although we haven't yet decided what to call a cold "hot tub"!

A pool - even a small one - seems to be more necessary if you plan to let out your finca when you're not using it yourself, and the higher rental that results will help to repay the installation cost. But remember that you do need permission to install a pool in Spain. It's seldom denied but will involve a delay which you should allow for. Also bear in mind that pools involve maintenance and running costs, even during those times when you are absent. For example, a 1KW circulation pump consumes about €50-worth of electricity per month, quite apart from the chemicals needed.

CHAPTER 15

BATTENING DOWN THE HATCHES

Water deposits. Predicting the storms, Emergency cooking, heating, lighting. Keeping out the elements. Problems with the track.

Most of the time, you can rely on Spain's hot sunshine blazing down on you from a clear or lightly clouded sky. That, after all, is one of the main attractions of the place. Any rain that may fall between May and September is usually in the form of a short, sharp shower, followed by a rapid return to the very pleasant norm.

Even during the winter months it is often equally bright and clear. Occasionally it's really, really nice, and on one memorable occasion we swam in the Med in early February. Also, being rather closer to the equator than more northern latitudes, the hours of winter daylight are still respectably long.

However, up in the mountains of Spain (as in mountainous areas elsewhere) the weather can suddenly and unexpectedly take a turn for the worse. Climbers and trekkers are regularly warned about this danger. If you are living in such areas, these adverse conditions can affect your ability to work, travel, cook, communicate or relax.

It is therefore important to do all you can to anticipate such conditions, and to prepare for them in advance so that your daily life is relatively unaffected during the short periods when they occur.

The opposite problem arises during the summer, when there can be up to seven months of high temperatures and little or no rainfall. Then you'll be faced with the possibility of water cuts and restrictions; or, if your supply comes from a well, this may dry up.

None of these problems are new, although some may claim that global warming is making them more severe. Countless generations who have suffered from these conditions in the past have devised ways of coming to terms with them, and you can do likewise.

The water supply

You might believe, in your innocence, that payment for water would entitle you to a regular supply. Not so in Spain. In the more remote parts of the campo, this service may be disrupted or restricted - usually as the result of prolonged drought, occasionally storms or floods, or sometimes for no apparent reason whatsoever. In some areas, in fact, water can only be piped through to you on a rota basis. This should not come as a surprise when you consider that Spain is supposedly the most mountainous and barren country in the EU.

The water deposit

It is therefore well worth making provision for some sort of reserve supply, known as a *depósito*. This was originally a concrete-lined hole in the ground, and newcomers to rural life in Spain often wonder why there should be so many strange swimming pools without steps or a filtration system. More recently, many people started building above-ground tanks from bricks or concrete blocks lined with cement, but nowadays large round plastic tanks are more commonly used. Prices start at about €75. If you live on a steeply sloping site and this can be located at the highest possible point, with the bottom of the tank higher than any point in the plumbing system, you should be able to avoid the need for a pump for your cold supply. However, such an arrangement is unlikely to produce sufficient pressure to trigger a gas water heater into action when the tap or shower is turned on.

Depending upon your needs, you can either regard your *depósito* as an emergency reserve to be streamed into your domestic system only when needed, or use it as a constantly replenished cistern for your daily domestic needs (apart from one tap for drinking water which will be connected directly to the mains supply).

In either case, the water enters - usually via a plastic supply pipe - through a regulating valve at the top of the *depósito*, with the outlet at the bottom.

As the *depósito* must be located as high as possible, it is often placed on a raised platform, supported by four pillars of square-section building blocks. To keep the water inside pure and free from bacteria and algae for as long as possible, the tank must have a well-fitting lid, normally secured by a chain or strap.

If you have a problem with sediment in your water, you can connect the tank in such a way that it also acts as a sediment trap. This entails connecting the output a short distance above the bottom of the tank, with a further tap at the bottom to allow any sediment to be flushed out at intervals as necessary.

Obviously water which is stored for any length of time in a warm climate will soon become unfit for drinking, So, whether or not you have a *depósito* fitted, we would strongly advise you to assemble a few large plastic cans (available at low cost from any hardware shop) which you can store in a cool place and replenish on a regular basis, ready for emergency use.

It is worth repeating that a water pressure gauge will usually give you some advance warning of a supply cut, by indicating a fluctuation in pressure long before you can otherwise detect this. This will enable you to ensure that all available cans and buckets are filled in readiness.

Predicting the Storms

As your daily life is likely to be disrupted by severe storms, it is worth doing all you can to predict them in advance. We have found weather forecasts to be of limited use in southern Spain, as the weather varies greatly over relatively short distances, and no two sources of meteorological information ever seem to agree. It's worth buying a barometer, as a strong wind is always preceded by a sudden drop (or even a rise) in pressure, but the actual pressure reading can be misleading - in Spain, you can have a long period of low pressure during the summer without the weather suffering in any way!

The secret to weather forecasting, we have decided, lies in a combination of watching the barometer and the wind direction. In our area, a shift to the north-west, accompanied by a steeply falling (or rising) barometric pressure always indicates the onset of a serious gale, while a north-easterly from the snow-capped Sierra mountains is the coldest. Warm, gentle south-easterly breezes and a high pressure bring African weather to the mountains, but if this wind direction changes to the west and pressure starts to fall, serious rain may be on its way. Strong winds are not always cold, of course, and an equally forceful hot breeze can also be quite a nuisance.

As the wind direction is such an influential factor, we decided to make an appropriately corazon-shaped weather vane and fit it to a redundant TV mast on the roof, with a ball bearing movement to make it sensitive to the slightest shift in wind direction. This was fun to make and watch, but we soon learned that winds tend to follow the direction of the deepest valley, and a more accurate indication of the direction from which weather is coming can be ascertained by watching the passing clouds!

Because our finca is located between the sometimes snow-capped sierras and the warm Mediterranean, the temperature can vary dramatically when the wind changes direction. We therefore made this simple "Corazon" style weathervane to give an early indication of change.

Emergency cooking and heating

Gas is more usual for both cooking and heating in the campo, which means that you can have a reserve supply on hand at all times. If you prefer to cook by electricity, make sure you have a readily-accessible alternative. A small camping gas cooker would be ideal for this purpose.

We must also repeat the wisdom of having more than one source of room heating. In our case we have three: electricity (convector heaters), gas (portable heater) and wood (our pot-bellied wood-burning stove, and the open fire).

Emergency lighting

Emergency lighting is another important consideration, and is frequently needed during the more severe winter storms. This may not need to be anything sophisticated - a good torch and a few strategically placed candles are quite sufficient for a cosy evening - but if you need to read, cook or even work from home then you'll need something better. A camping gas lantern, Tilley lamp or hurricane lamp are useful, but the ideal solution is to install a solar panel on the roof.

This panel trickle-charges one or more 12 volt car batteries throughout each day, which is used to power a few 12-volt 20-watt halogen dichroic reflector lamps (or, in fact, any type of 12 volt car bulb). The battery doesn't need to have an enormous capacity - a 48 amp-hour battery would run a couple of 20 watt lamps for 28 hours, or for a week at four hours an evening.

Thunderstorms can be quite violent in the mountains, and often affect the power supply. "Spikes" which can destroy electronic equipment are inevitable because of the countless miles of exposed, high-altitude supply cable and pylons. During a recent storm, which climaxed in a simultaneous lightning flash and crash of thunder, our power points lit up bright blue - and we imagine you can't have a bigger "spike" than that! Fortunately nothing sensitive was plugged in at the time, and the main switch "tripped" before much damage was done.

When such conditions are threatened, unplug all mains-operated electronic equipment (including any telephone). Surge protecting devices are useful, especially for those items that have to be permanently connected; a surprisingly large number of modern electrical appliances have built-in electronics which can be affected.

Think positive. A torrential downpour gives you the rare opportunity to identify all those elusive leaks! If rain regularly enters at the bottom of a window, look for a blocked drainage hole, or a weatherboard which does not overlap the outer frame. (Appropriately enough, we are writing this during one such power cut, by the light of a paraffin lamp. Thank goodness for the laptop computer, with its built-in battery!)

Keeping out the elements

The Spanish climate may be unusually pleasant but you can't expect every day to be perfect. Prepare for the worst and you won't be caught out.

The outside temperature in the winter may rarely fall to freezing, apart from the very occasional ground frost, but even if it's a mere five or six degrees higher than that it can feel distinctly uncomfortable in a stiff breeze. That's when every little draught in your home makes itself felt, as the inside temperature tries its hardest to equal that of the outside. Draught-proofing is the essential first step if you want to keep your finca reasonably warm, and you'll find out the best way to incorporate this in Chapter 9.

Taking delight in demolishing the dreaded doorstep, which persistently channelled water indoors instead of keeping it out, producing a permanently damp kitchen floor and wall.

Front doors in Spanish villages are often designed in a very strange way. There is an outside step that is designed to keep out the rain and draught, and this extends above the bottom of the inwards-opening door. It doesn't take a rocket scientist to fathom out that the rain running down the door is then able to travel down the vertical gap and straight into the front room, and it is common practice in the villages to cover the bottom of the front door with a sheet of plastic (not that this has much effect). Many people even go to the added insanity of boring a hole through the bottom of their front step so that the accumulated indoor puddle can drain back outside!

Much as we would have preferred keeping this quaint tradition alive in our own finca, we became so tired of sweeping the rain out through the front door that we decided on a more logical approach. The offending step was demolished. Immediately below the outer bottom edge of the door there is now a drop of a centimetre or so to the patio, which slopes away from the doorway. The rain runs off the door, down the drop and harmlessly away outside.

The track

The track leading to and passing by our finca and many others—following a sudden storm which made it almost impassable in a normal small car. Be prepared for such eventualities; in our case we make a point of parking above the problem area when bad weather threatens.

We have the feeling that problems with small tracks leading to remote fincas are becoming worse. This is possibly due in part to the more severe weather conditions that seem be part of global warming, but we are sure it can be largely blamed on the recently increased ploughing and chemical weed-killing of steep mountain slopes for crops, especially vines.

This type of cultivation removes the natural vegetation that used to bind the soil together, causing it to slide down on to the tracks and beyond, carrying the track with it. The heavier wear from the lorries of builders' merchants on tracks designed for mules is also a factor.

A major disruption of the main access track once happened to us during a violent storm, just as we were about to drive to the airport, and our only alternative route through a shallow ford was cut off by a raging torrent. In the end, after wasting an hour, the only answer was to brave the storm and repair the missing portion of track, using pickaxes and a boot full of rocks, until it was possible to leap across in the car.

Your land may include a rocky gully leading to or across a track, and this will probably look quite innocuous during the dry season. However, it will become unrecognisable during a flash flood. The further down the mountain it is, the greater will be the amount of water it carries at such times.

If you own the land on both sides of the track, it is often possible to sink large concrete drain sections beneath the track and channel the water harmlessly under the track. This should be done by an experienced builder who will have access to the necessary heavy lifting and digging equipment. However, it is rarely necessary for you to bear such expense yourself, as rural tracks are maintained with the help of a convenient EU grant and, sooner or later, the local council usually sorts the matter out.

Footnote

Reading through these warnings at a final proof-reading stage reminds us just how unpredictable the Spanish climate can be, which we suppose is one of its attractions. At this moment the radio is complaining of no real rain for the past seven months, with the associated risk of campo fires and a threat of serious water shortage before long!

CHAPTER 16

CAMPO RATIONS

Harvesting, eating or preserving prickly pears, olives and almonds. Using oranges and lemons. Using a bread oven.

This isn't a cookery book and so we won't be dealing with the wonderful local dishes like *paella*, or the selection of tasty *tapas* that you find in many bars. Instead we will be explaining how you can harvest, preserve and use the most common crops you are most likely to find growing around your finca, such crops as olives, almonds and prickly pears. And in case you want to know how the bread oven works, we will include a description of the technique for baking bread in one of these.

Peeling a prickly pear

Unlike many "foreign" fruit, prickly pears do not have what is politely described as an "acquired taste." They are absolutely delicious. In fact we are convinced that they would be very popular but for the drawbacks that they have to be handled with extreme care, and they do not keep well after picking. However, they have a surprisingly long season from about August to the end of October, and are quite easy to peel if you go about it in the correct way as follows.

Flowers and fruit of the prickly pear—tricky to peel but delicious to eat.

We pick them with barbecue tongs, which are also used when peeling. As the fruit ripens it changes from green to yellow, orange and red. We prefer the green fruit with a hint of yellow, as the seeds (which you normally eat) are larger in the ripest fruit. Holding the fruit in the tongs, cut off each end about 1cm down, and make a light diagonal cut from top to bottom. Lift one corner of the flap of skin with the point of the knife, then place the fruit in a shallow bowl. Grasp the flap of skin with the tongs, using the back of the knife to hold the fruit down, and the peel will come completely off.

Locals have a somewhat bolder technique that we have never mastered. They pick the fruit by wrapping it in a leaf or piece of cloth, then rub it on some rough grass to remove the spines, before holding it in their hand to peel it. When we try this method, we always seem to end up with some of the tiny glochids embedded in our hand, so we cannot wholeheartedly recommend it.

As well as eating them raw, you can make juice and syrup from prickly pears, blend them into milk shakes and smoothies, or add them to jams and preserves. Oddly enough, the flattened stems (known as "paddles" or *nopales*) can also be eaten, and they feature in some spicy Mexican dishes. We suspect that they would need disguising beneath a generous helping of chilli sauce before we would be tempted to try them.

In a really prolonged and baking hot summer drought, prickly pears can suffer badly. These tough and invasive plants, usually considered to be totally drought-proof, can then become limp and shrivelled. The fruit softens and drops to the ground before reaching the edible stage, producing a sickly odour while rotting which frequently attracts hordes of wasps to the area. The plants themselves usually recover with the return of the rains in the autumn, but the crop is lost.

Prickly pear clumps are associated with one undesirable aspect. They are traditionally used as dumps for household waste, particularly non-degradable things like glass bottles, paint tins and beer cans. If yours is beside a track, it may collect more than its fair share from passers-by.

Preserving olives

Olives are tricky things to preserve as they need extended treatment to remove their bitter taste. This is usually in brine. A solution of lye (caustic soda) is sometimes used, as this has a much more rapid action, but this substance is very corrosive and tricky to handle.

If you look up "preserving olives" on any internet search engine, you'll find dozens of recipes. Many of them are too sketchy to be of much help, but here's one that works:

Pick your olives for preserving just at the point when they are starting to turn purple. This will be quite early in November, four or five weeks before the main olive harvest in our area. Leave the stones in, but prick each olive just once with a fork. Soak in a solution containing 5% rock salt, and change this regularly - preferably on a daily basis.

After two to three weeks, taste an olive and if the bitterness has just about gone, soak them for a further day in 10% salt solution. Finally preserve them in a final solution. One way is to use a stronger version of the same, stronger saline solution can be used, to which you can add various herbs (especially oregano, garlic, cumin seeds, capsicums, red peppers or dill) and finish off with a top layer of olive oil.

However, we found that those we stored in the alternative way - in olive oil, flavoured with garlic, rosemary and orange peel - lasted better. The flavour of the resulting olives was every bit as good as commercial olives, but they were softer in texture. We haven't had as much success so far with preserving green olives, but we'll try some different techniques next season.

There are numerous ways of preserving olives, and the technique also varies with the variety and colour of the olive. It's a fascinating subject and well worth exploring on the internet, where you will find sites giving literally dozens of different recipes for Greek-style, lye-cured, water-cured or saline cured techniques.

Your almond harvest

Almonds are usually harvested during October, but this will vary according to the location and growing conditions. The less accessible nuts are dislodged by a long cane on to a net or cloth beneath. You can easily expect to harvest a good bucketful of almonds from a mature tree. A marketable weight of nuts can fetch from €1 to €1.50 per kilo (in 2003).

The first step is to remove the outer green husks; locals use a machine (often shared communally), but it's quite easy by hand if the husks are still green. The nuts can be stored for Christmas and beyond, but they're at their best when freshly picked, and make a pleasant accompaniment to a glass of fino. We find that it's quicker to crack them with a hammer than using nutcrackers.

If you want to try something different, which makes the nuts even more appetising, here's a simple recipe which we can recommend from Saxa Salt:

Mix together in a bowl:

1 egg white

1 teaspoonful of olive oil

1 teaspoonful of Saxa salt.

Add a large cupful of almonds and shake together in a polythene bag until evenly coated. Spread on a baking sheet and cook in a pre-heated oven at 120F (250F) or gas Regulo 3 for 15 minutes until golden brown. Store in screw-top jars.

Before using your almonds for cake making, or in order to make them more attractive for the table, they can be blanched. Cover them with boiling water until the skins are readily removed, then plunge into cold water before drying.

Oranges and Lemons

People tend to group these together and mention them in the same breath, but in cropping terms they are very different. Oranges have a distinct harvesting period in early spring, whereas lemons crop steadily over quite a long period - with blossom and fruit commonly appearing simultaneously.

Seville oranges - the bitter type used in marmalade making - are regarded as ornamental trees, and very often the fruit is left on the tree to rot. In our village, children use those growing in the square outside the Ayuntamiento as missiles in mock fights. If (like us) you're keen on making "real" marmalade, you should be able to get permission to pick all you need. Any you can't use straight away can be frozen. Proper preserving pans aren't easy to find in Spain, by the way, and other types of large saucepan aren't nearly as effective for marmalade making, so you may need to take one out with you. Lemon marmalade is also very refreshing, and can be made over a longer season.

Using a bread oven

Outside bread ovens are so commonly encountered in old fincas that we will add a few words on using them. If the bricks at the front are loose or crumbling apart, replace these first. Check the inside dome, which should be reasonably solid and intact. The floor of the oven should be sound and clean, as the loaves are placed directly on to this. It is not unknown for wandering cats or dogs to shelter inside a bread oven on a stormy night (a feral cat gave birth to her litter in ours!), so we suggest scrubbing it out first.

Do not expect to find a chimney anywhere, as this is unusual and the smoke normally comes out of the front during the heating phase. This may sound rather crude and basic, but you will probably be surprised at the efficient way in which such a design heats up, drawing in air from the bottom third of the opening and expelling the smoke from the top.

Carry out a test firing by lighting some dry sticks inside the oven. A small amount of smoke escaping from the roof is acceptable, but if this leakage is too great you will quickly lose the oven's heat and it would be advisable to render these bricks (which can be done on the outside, for ease of application, if you have access to the dome).

In our part of Andalucía, bread ovens are usually built outside. Ours was at the point of collapse and needed careful repair before it could be used.

You will also need to make an oven door to retain the heat, although you may be fortunate enough to find the original cover in an outhouse. This could be of iron or even made from a fairly substantial piece of hardwood, and you will need to improvise a means of supporting it in place - even if this is just a broomstick propping it up.

Prepare your dough in the usual way (making sure you specify that the flour must be "hard", i.e. intended for bread making), and follow the normal rising and kneading procedure while you light the fire for the final baking. This is done with faggots of sticks. We used bundles of small eucalyptus branches that had been gathered after a stormy night and dried in the shed, and these were ideal. We didn't even need any paper to start it off - a single match and it was away. Larger sticks were added to keep the fire going for about four hours. After that time, you will notice that the soot on the inside of the dome has turned a light grey.

Rake out the ashes and clean the bricks with an improvised gadget - say a bundle of wet leaves, heather or rushes tied to a broomstick. This is a messy business and it is wise to avoid inhaling the cloud of steaming ash that results. Then prop the door back into place and wait for the dust and steam to disperse and the temperature to stabilise, which can take up to an hour.

It should then have dropped to an even, overall temperature of around 450°F (230°C); you can use an oven thermometer if you have one, or you can use the traditional way to check this by tossing some unbleached white flour on to the bricks. If it takes about fifteen seconds for this to turn brown, it is time to put in the loaves and replace the door.

The tool used to insert and remove the loaves is called a paddle, and looks exactly like a flat-bladed boat paddle. We were fortunate enough to buy an antique paddle from a car boot sale in the UK, and took this out with us. If you need to make one we suggest using hardwood such as oak, as this is more fire-resistant, or you could fit a metal blade to a two-metre length of pole or tubing.

The risen dough will bake in anything from fifteen minutes upwards, depending on its size - baguettes are obviously ready much sooner, as are small rolls. It's also perfectly possible to bake pizza bread in one of these bread ovens. For more regular use, our breadmaking machine which we mentioned earlier is used on a daily basis and is one of our most valued possessions, saving us many unnecessary shopping trips to the village when all we really need is a loaf of bread.

CHAPTER 17

LIVING IN THE CAMPO

Making friends. Internet contact. Meeting the neighbours. How would you feel? Integrate yourself. Living with the wildlife. Gaining (and avoiding) pets. Dealing with pests. Learning the language. Translation programs.

Having spent so long finding, buying and renovating your finca, you'll want to make the best possible use of it.

Making friends

Living in a place that could be two or three kilometres from the nearest permanent occupant isn't exactly conducive to a busy social calendar, especially when those neighbours don't even share a common language. It's therefore not surprising that ex-pats tend towards the company of one another under such circumstances, if only to share their problems and experiences of living in their adopted country.

But it's not always easy to meet others of your own nationality, as they will also be tucked away in isolated locations in the campo. It's often possible to start up a conversation in the places where you are most likely to encounter them - particularly in the bank or post office, in the office of the local property agent, at the newsagents that distribute the free English-language papers, at the school if you have children there, or at the builder's merchant or hardware store.

If you are still unable to make contact, you could always make the first move by asking if you could display a notice in the post office or other shop windows, or in the nearest internet café if one exists, suggesting a get-together at a certain time and place - say a local bar. Our builder and his wife thoughtfully arranged such a meeting which proved a great success.

Internet contact

The internet, and its associated mailing groups and chat sites, are another place to make contact with like-minded people. There are Yahoo e-mail discussion groups covering principally ex-pats on the Costa-del-sol, Costa Blanca and the Almeria coast, and it costs nothing to join these and make contact with others with similar interests. See also the website www.fincabook.com, which contains details of these and other groups, as well as providing its own bulletin board.

Life in the campo is certainly different from the costa in many ways, and adjustments have to be made. While many ex-pats manage perfectly well in a seaside apartment without speaking a word of Spanish, they would need to learn the basics of the language fairly quickly if they were to move to a remote finca, with no English speakers in the nearest village.

Another difference is that you will almost certainly need to have a car of your own when there's a long track between you and the nearest loaf of bread or bottle of water. Indeed, if that track has a surface that is less than perfect, a four-wheel drive vehicle is likely to be needed, particularly during or after the winter storms.

Meeting the Spanish

Sooner or later, your Spanish neighbours are almost certain to visit you, introduce themselves and take great interest in looking around a house that they have probably known for most of their lives, so prepare yourself with the basic phrases of greeting. The fact that you're making an effort to communicate will be really appreciated by them. Most Spanish people, even in the depths of the countryside, are surprisingly formal in this respect, and it is worth swatting up on the standard expressions that are used so that you are prepared.

One such visitor to our finca, a kindly old man, turned up early one morning while we were both still in our pyjamas. Our attempts to communicate appeared to be even less successful than usual, until we realised that he was also very hard of hearing. Trying to speak a foreign language at high volume just inches from someone's ear isn't easy.

Having wandered inside and taken a close look around our untidy, partially demolished finca, we ushered him out with the excuse that we wanted him to point out where he lived. On the way to the high viewpoint on top of our mountain, he picked a ripe prickly pear and showed us how to peel it in an ingenious way that avoided without getting thorns stuck in our hands, which we really appreciated.

While he was pointing out his own house, we heard a donkey braying in the distance. Thinking that it might be his own animal, as the sound came from that direction, we asked if he had heard the *burro*, but our words fell quite literally on deaf ears. So we mimicked a donkey, raising our hands above our hands like large ears, and shouting "ee-aw, ee-aw" at the tops of our voices.

It only occurred to us later, when he had gone, that any passer-by must have been rather surprised to see two Brits in pyjamas at the top of a mountain mimicking a donkey.

The Spanish have a natural curiosity and friendliness that takes a reserved Englishman by surprise. We're also struck by their acceptance that queues are things to be enjoyed, a chance to catch up with the gossip and meet old friends, which contrasts with our former impression of the Mediterranean temperament as being rather volatile and impatient.

One recent example is typical. Finding that the deeply cut pruning blade supplied with the bow-saw we had bought was too rough for sawing up dry logs, we took it back to the village hardware store and asked if they had a finer toothed blade. Immediately we were asked by another customer exactly why the original blade was unsuitable, as he used his for pruning his almond trees with perfect satisfaction.

We had to try and explain, in our faltering Spanish, that we did not want to use it for pruning the soft wood of fruit trees, but for sawing up hard, dry eucalyptus trunks into logs. Had there been others in the shop at the time, we are quite sure they would all have joined in the discussion on the rights and wrongs of saw blades.

How would you feel?

We are constantly being surprised by the friendliness and courtesy of the local people. Sometimes we try to put ourselves in their shoes and imagine how we might feel in our home country if the situation were reversed. We try to picture a scenario in which our village in the UK suddenly became popular with foreigners who spoke no English and tended to group together, kept different hours, listen to their own radio stations and read their own newspapers. Would you feel kindly disposed towards such an invasion? All the more reason to remember that we are guests in a foreign country, and that it's well worth making every possible effort towards trying to learn the language and being as friendly and helpful in return as possible.

Integrate yourself

Without being too obvious about it, try to play a small but worthwhile part in your local community. As elsewhere, the secret is to give rather more than you receive, and this is not as difficult to arrange as you might imagine. Surplus produce should always be shared with your neighbours rather than allowed to go to waste. If the track which passes your finca suffers badly from a sudden storm, make sure you're one of the first to be out there with pick-axe and shovel, filling in the potholes. Take the trouble to keep your land free from vigorous weeds which might spread and annoy others. Make sure your place always looks as smart and tidy from the outside as we're sure it is within. If you want to be really public-spirited, build a small concrete trough beside the track which passes your land, and fill it regularly with drinking water for passing mules. And always be ready to lend a hand if a passing vehicle breaks down, or a stranger needs a glass of water - the word soon gets around, and it won't be long before you notice an even more friendly attitude towards you by the local population.

Living with the wildlife

What could be more enjoyable than relaxing in your own garden that just happens to be a natural wild-flower meadow?

If you want to make a success of living in the campo you must try to exist alongside nature, rather than force it into total submission. By all means make life more comfortable for yourself by tackling any major annoyances, such as large numbers of stinging or biting insects, but learn to live with things that don't harm or threaten you in any way.

We described the geckoes in an earlier chapter - little lizard-like creatures with pads on their feet, that keep down the fly and spider population inside your house. They are delightful in almost every way and really deserve your protection and encouragement.

Most of the other wildlife you will come across is equally benign. Crickets may make their presence very obvious on a balmy summer's night, but would the place be the same without their evocative background music? The same applies to those strange Scop's Owls, with a nocturnal call sounding just like an electronic beacon.

Although we know they exist, we have yet to find a single scorpion lurking beneath an upturned stone, and we have not come across any (fortunately rare) venomous snakes of any size. The presence of mosquitoes, gnats, midges and wasps varies with location and season, but there certainly seem to be fewer of these bugs on top of a mountain than in the damp and still air of lower regions.

The only animals you will certainly encounter are the free-ranging dogs of the campo. These are unlikely to cause you any harm as they are invariably timid creatures. It's rather exciting to know that Spain still contains eagles, vultures, wolves and wild boar. Although you are less likely to encounter these in everyday life, we once came across a local hunt which had just killed no less than six wild boar, only a couple of kilometres from our finca.

There is however one aspect of rural Spain that can cause unexpected problems. Be careful about walking through areas of long grass; dry seed heads from certain types of grasses can work their way through socks and irritate the skin. Also beware of disease-carrying ticks, which are a particular danger to dogs and, sadly, I have known them to be fatal in some cases.

Gaining (or avoiding) pets

Soon after you settle in the campo, it is likely that an assortment of underfed dogs will appear on your doorstep with an appealing "please look after me" look in their eyes. They seem to have the uncanny knack of sensing the arrival of foreigners, whom they know to be a "soft touch".

Some of these dogs will belong to local finca owners who normally live in a nearby village. They will be fed from time to time -

sometimes only at weekends and on the occasional weekday evening - and so they are always on the lookout for something to supplement their meagre diet.

Others could be genuine campo strays - poor half-starved wretches, often injured or diseased, living out a hapless existence by scavenging for food from rubbish dumps and household bins. And you may even have some young (or not-so-young) dogs or cats brought to you by the owner, knowing that foreigners are more likely to be tempted to offer them a home.

Try and agree a firm policy regarding pets in advance - and stick to it. This sounds fine in theory, until you meet that one pair of soulful eyes that you simply can't resist.

Dealing with insect pests

There are few really troublesome pests in the Spanish campo, and these seem to be less prevalent in exposed places and occur mainly during the high summer months. However, quite a few flies seem to find their way indoors, both the annoying smaller type and a few of the larger and noisier blow-flies. Once the summer fly-screens are up at the windows (and the windows themselves are kept closed for a greater part of the day) they become less of a problem.

Mosquitoes at night can be annoying, particularly on very warm nights when you need the minimum of covering on the bed. The problem doesn't justify using a tropical-style mosquito net over the bed, so you need to pay scrupulous attention to the fitting of window screens and to keeping doors closed.

If you are sufficiently bothered to consider spraying the room, make sure you read (and understand) the invariably Spanish instructions on the can, as most of the effective sprays sound rather hazardous and demand thorough airing before the room can be occupied (which rather seems to defeat the object of the spraying). The time we find sprays most useful is when leaving the house unoccupied, as it keeps any build-up of pests to the minimum.

We have found the small plug-in tablet heaters to be very effective, as they seem to work even with the windows open. Products based on citronella oil and other natural extracts are supposed to be effective deterrents, but these work for some people and not for others.

Older methods of pest control are available which are, on the whole, more environmentally friendly. Don't overlook the humble fly-swatter, which is both cheap and effective, as are fly-papers. It is also a sound policy to encourage geckoes into your home, those delightfully acrobatic house lizards that have a voracious appetite for all insects.

We are visited by those strange creatures that we have nick-named "shaking spiders". Measuring up to 10cm (4 inches) across, they have small round bodies and spindly legs on which they "bounce" up and down when disturbed. As we mentioned earlier, these seem to originate from the bamboo ceiling of our stable during the summer, migrating to other parts of the house and sometimes forming themselves into large clusters. They are susceptible to the large cans of insect spray sold by most supermarkets, but this chemical is potent stuff and the instructions (usually in Spanish) must be carefully followed, particularly with respect to the need for airing rooms before re-occupation. However, we are sure this pest will disappear for good now that its favourite habitat is firmly encased in concrete and plaster! Other occasional nuisances include earwigs and woodlice, but they don't do any real harm; they are probably only noticeable after the house has been unoccupied for a few weeks, when they tend to accumulate in the various nooks and crannies.

Rodent pests

We have been troubled by mice from time to time. One in particular used to sneak out of the stable and squeeze under our bedroom door into the kitchen at the same time every evening, leaving the inevitable and undesirable calling cards in the kitchen during the night.

Having studied its habits and traced its exact route over several nights, we decided that the best solution was to block its path so that it could not escape from the stable in the first place. So we screwed a strip of wood firmly to the bottom of the stable door, leaving not the slightest crack that would allow it to squeeze through.

That night, the mouse kept us awake for many hours while it attempted, unsuccessfully, to chew and scratch its way through the door. In the end, in sheer desperation, I stumbled out of bed and opened the door to allow it through, after which we lapsed into peaceful sleep. Mouse one, humans nil. After that we resorted to poison, we're afraid. I suppose it worked, eventually, as our mouse was no longer evident.

On one occasion we were visited by a large brown rat, which proved to be far more destructive, chewing up curtains and a new rug. This pest succumbed to our poison treatment within a few days and we were reassured to discover its body under the sink. Jesús, whose local store supplied the poison, suggested that a 50/50 mixture of flour and Yeso plaster was also reputed to be very effective!

Try to get the most out of living in Spain by taking an interest in local festivities. This was taken at the Easter Passion Play in Riogordo, in which most of the village plays a part, and shows Jesus preaching to the multitude.

215

Serious language learning

Whereas one may be able to get along quite happily with little or no Spanish in the ex-pat enclaves of the Costa, learning the language becomes a virtual necessity if you decide to live in or near a village where no English is spoken.

Apart from anything else, the local people will appreciate the trouble you take to learn their language, and they respond accordingly. So one of your first priorities - preferably before you even start looking for somewhere to renovate or live in - should be to make a really serious effort to learn Spanish.

There are many different ways to learn the language, and none is outstandingly superior to the others. What is far more important is the time and effort you put into the task of learning. You can learn from educational TV programmes, from audio tapes, video cassettes, books, internet websites or interactive CD-ROMs. You can attend day or evening Adult Education courses at local schools and centres in your home country, or Spanish for Foreigners classes in Spain at four different levels, run by the *Escuela Official de Idiomas* - a whole term at 8 hours a week can cost as little as €48, and they are often recommended by those who have tried them. The phone number for the one in Málaga is 952 27 20 07 or 952 27 25 02.You can also join a commercially run class, in the UK or in Spain, or you can take private lessons in most towns and villages, on a one-to-one basis or by sharing the cost with your partner.

Another option is offered by the adult literacy and numeracy classes which run for a couple of hours daily in many larger villages. The class in Colmenar, for instance, runs daily from 9 a.m. to 11 a.m. and you can enrol at the beginning of any term. Several English residents have joined these classes and, although the tuition is entirely in Spanish, they report being made to feel very welcome and have found the classes extremely helpful.

While in the early stages of learning, we relied heavily on a few basic phrases that often brought results when we were trying to track down places and suppliers. "Por favor, donde esta..." will produce directions to your destination from a stranger; "donde puedo comprar..." may reveal where you can buy something you're having difficulty finding. In both cases, the main problem will be that you need to understand the reply. "¿Podria escribirlo?" (handing over a notepad and pen) should produce the answer in writing, which may be more helpful. "No hablo español" and "¿habla ingles?" are of course essential for the absolute beginner. Finally, whatever you say, try and remember to smile at the same time—which is easier said than done, but it really does make all the difference to the response you receive.

If you have problems with your vocabulary, we find that little "Post-it" notes displayed around the place can provide helpful reminders. As soon as you have gained a basic vocabulary, take every possible opportunity of using it. These may be rare when you're living way out in the campo, but employing local people (e.g. for building, domestic cleaning or gardening) is one way to get chatting to them - as of course is the very necessary acts of shopping or - probably best of all - having a haircut. If you're in a bar, don't be shy to break the ice; in every case, a brief comment on, say, the weather will indicate that you're keen to make contact and practise your Spanish.

One thing we have noticed is that our badly spoken Spanish is more likely to be understood by a well educated Spaniard, who we suppose is best able to make an "intelligent guess" at what we're trying to say; it's far more difficult to pass the time of day with a passing farmer, even though I'd be really interested to learn about his crops and benefit from his experience. Listening to Spanish radio and watching Spanish TV can help a little, and you'll eventually find yourself picking out more and more words.

Gradually you'll find that you've picked up enough of the various verbs, nouns and rules so that they begin to slot together like a jigsaw, and then the process of learning becomes a little easier.

Translation programs

My grasp of the language is still inadequate for involved correspondence with suppliers or detailed instructions to tradesmen, and we often have to rely on the automatic translation program on our laptop. Such programs can never be perfect, as many words in one language can have a number of quite different meanings in another, only one of which will be appropriate and the rest will make nonsense of the translation. However, by starting off with simple and unambiguous English, converting this to Spanish and then translating back again to double-check the result, we can usually avoid the more blatant mistakes, and the program has been absolutely invaluable on a number of occasions.

In one case we needed to explain to the garage owner which was storing our car while we were abroad that we would be arriving at Málaga airport that night well after midnight, and to ask if they could kindly leave the car just outside their locked gates when they closed for the night so that we could rendezvous by taxi? So we translated the request, rang Juan the garage owner, asked him to wait a moment, turned the translation program on to voice mode, held the phone against the speaker of our computer and played the synthesised Spanish translation to him. Afterwards, we asked him "¿entiende? comprende todo?" to which he replied "Si, si" with a laugh - and sure enough, there was our little old car sitting right outside his gates in the early hours of the next morning. Which was just as well, or I'd have been in a real fix.

It is even possible to scan a document, such an instruction leaflet or magazine article, run it through an OCR program which coverts it into a text file, and then translate this. Sometimes the results are amusing (I won't tell you how it translated the "5 anos garantia" for our toilet mechanism, which I had mistakenly typed without accents). However, reading Spanish is the easiest part of learning the language; speaking Spanish, understanding spoken Spanish, and writing in Spanish all take longer to master.

CHAPTER 18

KEEPING IN TOUCH

Avoiding unnecessary worries. Mobile phones - the cost of roaming. Spanish SIM cards. Unlocking your phone. Transferable numbers. Sending documents by E-mail and fax via your laptop and mobile phone. Making best use of an internet café.

Avoiding unnecessary worries

Few things are more frustrating than being back in your home country while your precious residence-to-be or holiday home is torn apart by an unseen and virtually unknown builder. You lie awake imagining the worst while roofs are stripped off, walls fall down, rubble builds up in the garden and the whole site is left exposed to the elements and to uninvited guests.

Problems grow in your mind and you may even start to doubt the expertise and integrity of your builder. It is therefore wise to choose a builder with whom you can not only communicate readily, but also to find a way in which you can keep in regular contact.

Ideally you'd be dealing with someone offering a fax, e-mail, digital camera and articulate English, but—let's face it—this just isn't going to happen. In our case we were fortunate enough to meet another English couple who were also in the middle of major building work, and who were staying on after we returned home. They were kind enough to keep us regularly supplied with progress reports by fax and even sets of photographs showing the latest developments. Some of these photographs are included in this book.

But what about communicating with friends, family or business colleagues on a regular basis when you're living in Spain? Or, for that matter, calling the many suppliers within Spain you may need to contact? As it's unlikely you'll be able to arrange a landline connection to a remote mountain finca (although it costs nothing to apply), you will probably be dependent on the mobile phone or local phone box. The signal for a mobile phone is usually good at higher altitudes, but problems are more common in the valleys.

It's certainly worth asking whether you can be connected to a normal telephone, even though Telefonica seem increasingly reluctant to install their radio telephone service to remote places. To check, dial 1004 from a friend's telephone or local call box, and ask for "Servicio Ingles".

The heavy cost of roaming

You have probably worked out by now that roaming abroad using a mobile phone from your home country is a frightfully expensive business. If your partner also has a mobile and you use them to keep in touch with each other while in Spain, you'll be paying something close to double the international mobile rate between you. Roaming on such a mobile is fine for occasional use, but it's worth thinking about getting your phone "unlocked" by your network, so that you can then insert a pre-pay SIM card you can buy in Spain. Alternatively, consider buying a replacement Spanish mobile based upon whichever network gives the strongest signal in your location.

If you do have to resort to roaming, either as a temporary measure or if you encounter problems unlocking your phone, there are ways of reducing the cost. You can choose to divert all calls to your mailbox, reducing call times and leaving you only with the collection charge to pay. Or you can ask callers to leave a message on a home-based answering machine, which you access remotely (at cheap rate) from your mobile.

International roaming does have one advantage, however, in that it can automatically select whichever of the Spanish networks gives the strongest signal at any time.

It's worth remembering that you can usually save quite a lot by using a local Spanish phone box, if you have one that's not too far away. We like the way you can ask the more modern boxes to display their instructions in English, and the way they can give change for unused portions of your payment. Some of the older boxes aren't averse to gobbling up your money without connecting you, though we are assured that a refund will be posted to you if you know enough Spanish to complain.

Transferrable numbers

You can register free of charge at www.yac.com (and certain other sites which also offer a transferable number service) and they will supply a single telephone number that can follow you around the world. Callers dialling this number are then connected to you at whatever number you have currently given to the company, wherever you may be in your own country or on the continent.

The calls cost the caller more than standard, to fund the service, but at weekends the charge is very reasonable and transfers currently cost no more to yourself or the caller, even when transferred to a Spanish mobile (though you would still pay a forwarding charge if you're roaming on your home network). Also, any fax messages sent to such a number can be scanned and sent to your e-mail address as a file attachment. You can change the forwarding number at any time (if you buy a new SIM card for instance), either by phone or through the website of the company concerned.

As in many other countries, services exist in Spain which offer reduced-rate calls (even to mobile phone users in some cases) after dialling a special prefix. The cost of the call is charged to your bank or credit card, or deducted from a deposit. You'll find such services advertised in the various free English papers and magazines which are distributed along the coast.

Sending documents and text home

Communications is a rapidly developing field and there are numerous ways in which you can send and receive messages, or connect to the internet:

- You could buy a mobile phone with a built-in modem and data cable, and use this to transmit your fax or e-mail by plugging in to a laptop or hand-held computer on which you have composed and saved the message. You could also use one of the reasonably priced little PDAs or a more expensive sub-notebook pocket PCs which makes the task even simpler. Then, for e-mail or internet access, you have these main options:

(a) Set up an account with a Spanish ISP, for which you will probably need to buy a Spanish mobile or to have your existing mobile "unlocked" and fitted with a Spanish SIM card.

(b) Use the pay-as-you-go service provided by many of the networks issuing your Spanish SIM card; a good mobile phone shop will help you download and install the software. Also consider GPRS which is quicker and more reliable.

(c) Dial in to the local node if you already subscribe to an international service such as AOL or Compuserve (although this might incur a hefty surcharge).

- If your laptop has a modem, whether built-in or external, you can send fax messages via a suitable mobile phone, or you could plug the serial cable in to a friend's landline telephone socket and send them that way. The advantage of a fax message is that the recipient knows immediately that you have sent a message, whereas an e-mail message can sit there for days until the computer is switched on and logged into the net. You'll also see a fax service offered at virtually all hotels, many stationery and office equipment shops, larger newsagents, a few cafes and bars, even occasionally in unlikely places such as garages, and you can get the best value from this service by composing your message on your computer and printing it out in a very small sized type.

- You can visit an internet cafe, access the internet or receive and send your e-mail via a Hotmail (www.msn.com) or Yahoo (www.yahoo.com) account, or via your existing service provider's website.

- Finally, any mobile phone can be used to send 160-character, low-cost text messages to another mobile anywhere in the world. This is one of the cheapest, quickest and best ways of keeping in touch, even when roaming. Contrary to popular belief, these messages are not passed on instantaneously, particularly when sending between different networks, but rarely take more than five or ten minutes to arrive. They can also be sent as e-mails or fax messages via various services offered by mobile phone networks and independent sources such as Yac.

E-mail with a mobile phone

If you do decide to send your e-mail to and from a mobile phone, and you have arranged an e-mail address with a facility such as Hotmail or Yahoo which you can access easily from anywhere in the world, you can set this up as your preferred e-mail account in Outlook Express (v.5 onwards), just as you would for any normal service provider. This enables you to compose off-line using Outlook Express, and then go on-line to send/receive your e-mail more quickly than it would otherwise take to log on to the Hotmail or Yahoo website. With Hotmail, we usually adjust our settings so that only incoming messages from people in our address list are immediately received, which speeds up access. This means that it we are able to connect, send and receive several messages within a total online time of only about three minutes, at an off-peak cost (March 2003) of only 18 to 24 cents, making e-mail via a mobile phone far more affordable.

The Internet Café

If you need to access your e-mail, send longer messages or get some information from a website and you don't know anyone who's connected to the net, you'll need to visit an internet café. These can be found in any of the larger towns and at airports. If you haven't used one before but know how to surf the web, you will very quickly feel at ease. Fortunately, most internet café staff speak English. The internet connection is often via satellite, giving quite rapid access, and the cost can be as little as €2 to €3 for a half-hour session.

You should, however, prepare yourself in advance by opening a Hotmail or Yahoo account (at www.msn.com or www.yahoo.com) or by finding out from your normal service provider how you can access your e-mail from another site. Having set up this facility, try it out at home before you leave. You can also save yourself time by transferring the most important e-mail addresses in your address book into that site in advance.

Many internet cafés run special software which is very user-friendly, offering a choice of sites and options at a single touch from the main menu, including direct access to the Hotmail and Yahoo sites, search engines and so on. You can often also log on and off as you wish, the total on-line time being recorded by a counter. Usually a printer is networked into the system, so that you can print messages or websites that you wish to keep, paying for these at a few cents per copy.

Some internet cafés allow you to upload text from a floppy disk, or images from a digital camera, but they may require you to scan for viruses first or impose other conditions. This is something you should discuss with them when you book in.

You should also ask in advance how to print a copy of any important messages and what the cost will be - if this is not prominently displayed, which it usually is. This price list may include many other services such as scanning and saving files on to floppy disks or even CD-ROMs.

Communications updates - see the Fincabook website

Communications is a field that is being continually developed, and there are some exciting new advances on the way which will give easier and quicker access via advanced types of mobile phone. We will keep you updated through the Fincabook website, www.fincabook.com.

CHAPTER 19

RESEARCHING ON THE INTERNET

Web sites with fincas for sale; general information/maps about areas of Spain; newspaper and magazine sites; learning the language; weather and webcams; free translations and other services. Bulletin Boards and E-mail discussion groups. Building and Restoration sites. Cheap travel.

Many friends and members of various e-mail groups have recommended websites to us, which we have compiled into this list. We have also included sites which we found useful in our research for this book. Some sites of them are portals or gateways which point the way to others of interest, so your armchair journey may become longer (and more enjoyable) than you first imagined.

Websites are notorious for becoming extinct or changing their URL, so if any of these are not available when you try them, an enquiry through a good search engine like www.google.com will usually locate alternative sources of the information.

We have also included details of several e-mail groups to which anyone who is living in Spain, or thinking of doing so, can join. Members of these groups are often able to answer any questions you may have, and they also offer an excellent way of making new contacts and friends.

Property sales
(sites including a proportion of older fincas)
www.cortijo-andalucia.com
www.countrypropertiesalora.com
www.escapetospain.co.uk
www.fincasandalucia.com—*Colmenar and surrounding areas*
www.green-blue.com/property_search.html
www.homesinspain.com
www.housesforsaleinspain.com—*Colmenar area*
www.interealtynet.com/british/PropertySearch
www.lostajos.com
www.propertyworldmagazine.com/search/index.htm—*searches their classified ads*
www.spain-homes.org
www.spainhomes.com
www.wessexhomes.com

Property sales
(mainly newer developments)
www.suncomfort.com/english/index.html
www.atecon.com/indice.htm
www.atriumreal.com/engelsk/start.htm
www.calahonda-estates.com
www.casamarbella.com
www.cielomijas.com
www.dse-spain.com/eng/index.htm
www.futursol.com
www.hiperprop.com
www.imagesofandalucia.com
www.immolink.net/inlink—*also covers Europe*
www.leiner.net
www.marbellalife.com—*combines Marbella area property with general information*
www.medestates.com
www.msinmo.com
www.pedevilla.com
www.properties.solweb.es
www.property-spain.com—*includes lots of general information*

www.ramondiz.com/main.htm
www.reluz.com/search.shtml
www.sirocoestates.com
www.solproperties.com
www.spanish-property-shop.com
www.sunshine-estates.com
www.villamarketing.com

Local and general information
(Portals to other sites etc)
www.hotcosta.com
www.puertobanus.info—*useful site of information and links*

Weather forecasts/reports
http://home.netscape.com/bookmark/40/weather.html
www.bbc.co.uk/weather.
www.weather.com—*printable 10-day forecast for major towns in Spain.*
www.wunderground.com/global/stations/08482.html—*a good site giving weather information and forecast for Málaga.*

Webcams
If your finca is up in the mountains and the weather is unsettled there, it can be worth taking a look at the current picture from the nearest webcam on the coast to see if the conditions are good enough to justify taking a trip there.
www.marbellalife.com/webcams/spain/index.html (then click on "Webcams")—*An excellent general site which includes other useful information and links.*

Local/general information
http://directory.google.com/Top/Regional/Europe/Spain
http://fullcoverage.yahoo.com/fc/World/Spain
http://potable.editthispage.com—*discussion site for drinking water problems in Spain*
http://travelinginspain.com/culture.html
www.altur.com—*comprehensive information on Andalucía*
www.adalucia.com
www.adalucia.org—*Andalusian Tourism Department official site, very comprehensive*

www.adalucia-online.net
www.cea.es—*Andalusian businesses*
www.costadelsol.net
www.dgt.es/index.html
www.directoryspain.com/costadelsol.shtml
www.docuweb.ca/SiSpain/
www.gti.ssr.upm.es/~vlmp/SPAIN—*full listing of museums and their speciality*
www.keytomijascosta.com—*about Mijas*
www.livinginspain.co.uk
www.marbella-guide.com, *and* www.marbella.com—*dedicated to Marbella*
www.spainalive.com
www.spainview.com—*detailed editorial and PR information on Spain*
www.spanishforum.org
www.typicallyspanish.com
www.uk.tourspain.es—*helpful practical touring advice in English*
www.unicaja.es—*site of a Spanish bank which holds information days for foreign residents*
www.visitcostadelsol.com—*official site of the Costa del Sol Tourist Board*

Driving in Spain

www.dgt.es/ientrada.html—*The Spanish Highway Code in English*
www.lhdplace.co.uk— *used left-hand drive cars in Basingstoke (UK) ready to export*
Building conservation, advice and grants
www.dirtcheapbuilder.com—*U.S. site on building with natural materials for the enthusiast*
www.icomos.org—*ICOMOS conservation organisation, France*
www.irishstonewalls.com—*technical, re stone wall restoration*
www.mikewye.co.uk—*traditional materials and advice*
www.northcoast.com/~tms/stone.html—*building with stone*
www.obrien.ie (Irish publisher)—*details of their technical books, including "Stone Buildings"*
www.past.demon.co.uk—*UK-based preservation organisation specialising in stone buildings*
www.tin.it—*European Centre for Conservation, Venice*

Harvesting and using crops

http://groups.yahoo.com/group/OliveOil/message/212—*olive varieties*
http://homecooking.miningco.com/food/homecooking/library/weekly/b
lbrining.htm —*recipes for curing olives*
www.desertusa.com/magoct97/oct_pear.html—*lots of prickly pear recipes*

Bulletin Boards

www.Andalucia.co—*also has a very active notice board, often with 20 or more follow-up replies to each posting*
www.docuweb.ca/Spain—*free display of sales, wants and contacts*

E-mail groups

fincasinspain-subscribe@yahoogroups.com
costa-del-sol-subscribe@yahoogroups.com
and almer-subscribe@yahoogroups.com
To join, send a blank email to any of the above. Yahoo will reply to your e-mail address, asking you to confirm your request for security reasons, after which you will begin receiving the postings. Normally you won't be inundated with messages, but—if a group becomes too popular—you can choose to receive a weekly list of subject headings. For more information on Yahoo groups, see http://groups.yahoo.com.

Searching for help

www.expatexpert.com—*advice on many aspects of living abroad*
www.google.com—*probably the quickest and most powerful search engine. Even entering your own name or post/zip code may produce some surprising results!*

Learning the language

www.diccionarios.com—*very comprehensive and even translates technical terms*
www.ectaco.co.uk/online—*online dictionary and translations*
www.freetranslation.com
www.learnspanish.com—*exactly what it says, much of it free*
The Google and Yahoo search pages also incorporate a useful website and text translation feature.

Newspapers and periodicals

www.autotrader.co.uk *or* www.exchangeandmart.co.uk—*you can search for a LDH car to drive there from the UK*

www.costadelsolnews.es

www.globuscom.es—*The site of the publishers of Casas Restauradas (Restored Houses) and Casa & Campo (House and Country); in Spanish*

www.streetwise-magazine.com—*Streetwise, free monthly magazine published in Nerja*

www.surinenglish.com—*excellent web version of the free weekly paper for expats, with good search facility on its classifieds*

www.theentertainer.net—*web version of the popular free newspaper on the coast.*

Getting there (cheap flights)

Fare vary enormously, by a factor of up to ten times, so it's worth spending a little time comparing the following:

www.air2000.com

www.avro.com

www.britanniadirect.com—*TUI UK Ltd., which incorporates Skydeals, Thomson etc.*

www.easyjet.com

www.ebookers.com

www.flightline.es—*with an office in Málaga airport*

www.flybe.com—*now incorporates the new service from Southampton airport*

www.flymonarch.com—*our particular favourite*

www.mytravel.com

www.ryanair.com

www.servitour.es—*with an office in Málaga airport*

www.thetravelshop.com—*travel shop with office in Malaga airport*

Bibliography:

CORTIJOS, HACIENDAS Y LAGARES, published by the Junta de Andalucía. ISBN 84-8095-271-7. A large coffe-table book in Spanish filled with photographs of old properties and village scenes.

JAVEA/XABIA: A YEAR IN THE LIFE OF A SPANISH TOWN, by Charlene Quince: ISBN 84-605-9704-0.

LIVING IN THE CAMPO by Maggie hutton, Bookworld, España.

LIVING AND WORKING IN SPAIN by David Hampshire: Survival Books, 0-9519804-2-3.

THE OXFORD-DUDEN PICTORIAL SPANISH DICTIONARY, a dictionary with a completely different approach: page after page of detailed technical drawings on every subject under the sun, from the building site to the human body, with every item identified. Our builder recommended it to us and we found it invaluable.

THE READER'S DIGEST COMPLETE DO-IT-YOURSELF MANUAL (the Reader's Digest Association Ltd., London): a clear introduction to the basics of bricklaying, concreting, tiling, plumbing and electrics.

STONE BUILDINGS by Patrick McAfee (1998): The O'Brien Press Ltd., Dublin. Includes useful information on the preparation and use of lime mortars and paints.

Periodicals:

CASA & CAMPO, c/Covarrubias, 1. 28010 Madrid. 222.globuscom.es. In Spanish, 3 euros per issue.

CASAS DE CAMPO, Pérez Galdos 36, 08012 Barcelona.

CASAS RESTAURADAS (Restored Houses), c/Covarrubias, 1. 28010 Madrid. 222.globuscom.es. In Spanish, 3 euros per issue.

GLOSSARY

Please bear in mind that different terms may be used in different areas of Spain.

English-Spanish

Acro prop	*puntal*
Acrylic	*acrílico*
Aggregate	*grava*
Arch	*arco*
Beam	*viga*
Bracket	*escuadra*
Bricks	*ladrillos*
Brick course	*hilada de ladrillos*
Cable	*cable*
Cement	*cemento*
Circular saw	*radial*
Chase	*regola*
Chip board	*aglomerado*
Coachbolt	*tornillo de cabeza redonda*
Cold chisel	*cincel*
Compresion fitting	*junta de compresión*
Concrete	*hormigón*
Concrete mixer	*hormigonera*
Conduit	*macarrón*
Copper pipe	*tornillo para madera*
Cracks	*grietas*
Dampness	*humedad*
Delivery charge	*pago de transporte*
Demolish	*derribar*
Distribution panel	*cuadro eléctrico*
Door frame	*marco de la puerta*
Door hinge	*bisagra*
Eaves	*aleros*
Entrance cable	*cable de entrada*

Estate agency	*agencia inmobiliaria*
Estimate	*presupuesto*
Extension lead	*alargadera*
Fine agrégate gravel	*grava fina*
Float	*plana*
Flux (soldering)	*empaste*
Foundations	*caballete*
Grants	*grava*
Grout	*lecheo*
Gutter bracket	*soporte de canalón*
Guttering	*canalización del tejado*
Gutter tiles	*tejas de canal*
Half inch thread (plumbing)	*rosca de 1/2 pulgada*
Hammer	*martillo*
Headers	*Aparejos*
JCB digger	*excavadora*
Junction box	*caja de conexiones*
Key	*anclaje*
Leak	*fuga de agua*
Light switch	*interruptor*
Lime	*cal*
Limewash paint	*pintura de cal*
Linseed oil	*aceite de linaza*
Lintel	*dintel*
Mason	*albañil*
Masonry drill	*broca*
Mattock	*raedera*
Measure	Regla
Miniature circuit breakers	*ICP*

Paint	*pintura*
Pincers	*tenazas*
Pitch (of a roof)	*pendiente* del tejado
Plane	*cepillo*
Planed lumber	*madera limpia*
Planning permit	*licencia de obras*
Plaster	*yeso*
Pliers	*alicates*
Pointing	*lecheo*
Power socket	*enchufe*
Pressure regulator	*regulador de presión*
Putty lime	*masilla*
Reinforcing mesh	*mallazo*
Rendering	*enlucido*
Ring beam	*zuncho*
Riser (of steps)	*contrahuella*
Roof beam	*viga del techo*
Roof pitch	*pendiente del tejado*
Roof tiles (top tiles)	*tejas superiores*
Rough cast wall finish	*terminación tosca*
Ruin	*ruina*
Rustic (rough)	*rústico*
Sagging roof	*tejado caído*
Sand	*arena*
Saw	*sierra*
Saw, metal	*sequeta*
Saw, wood	*serrucho*
Scraper flat	*palustre*
Scraper triangular	*palustre de lengua vaca*
Screwdriver	*destornillador*
Security lock	*cerradura de seguridad*
Septic tank	*pozo séptico*

Settlement cracks	*fisuras*
Sewer line	*saneamiento*
Shelf	*repisa*
Shovel	*pala*
Shuttering (for concrete)	*encofrado*
Shuttering (for arch)	*cercha*
Skip	*cuba, contenedor*
Sledge hammer	*mazo*
Spirit level	*nivel*
Stone and clay wall	*tapia*
Stretchers (bricks)	*hiladas*
Terracotta tiles	*lozas de barro*
Tile cutter	*cortadora de azulejos*
Title deed	*escritura de compra-venta*
Town Hall	*ayuntamiento*
Tread (of steps)	*peldaño*
Trowel	*palustra catalana*
Underpinning	*reforzado*
Varnish	*varniz*
Ventilator	*turbina*
Vice	*broca manual*
Wall plug	*taco*
Wall tie	*traba*
Washer	*arandela*
Waste pipe	*tubería de desagüe*
Waste trap	*bote sifónico*
Water storage tank	*depósito de agua*
Waterproof	*impermeable*
Wheelbarrow	*carretilla*
Window bars	*rejas*

Spanish-English

Aceite de linaza	linseed oil
Acrílico	acrylic
Agencia inmobiliaria	estate agency
Aglomerado	chip board
Alargadera	extension lead
Albañil	mason
Aleros	eaves
Alicates	pliers
Anclaje	key
Aparejos (bricks)	headers
Arandela	washer
Arco	arch
Arena	sand
Ayuntamiento	Hall
Barniz	varnish
Bisagra	door hinge
Bote sifónico	waste trap
Broca	masonry drill
Broca manual	vice
Caballete	gable end wall
Cable	cable
Cable de entrada	entrance cable
Caja de conexiones	junction box
Contrahuella	riser (of steps)
Cortadora de azulejos	tile cutter
Cuadro eléctrico	distribution panel
Cal	lime
Canalización del tejado	guttering
Carretilla	wheelbarrow
Cemento	cement

Cemento cola	tile cement
Cepillo	plane
Cerradura de seguridad	security lock
Cimentación	foundations
Cincel	cold chisel
Contenedor, cuba	skip
Escuadra	bracket
Depósito de agua	water storage
Derribar	demolish
Destornillador	screwdriver
Dintel	lintel
Empaste	flux (soldering)
Enchufe	power socket
Encofrado	shuttering
Escuadra	bracket
Enlucido	rendering
Escritura Compra-Venta	title deed
Excavadora	JCB digger
Fisura	settlement cracks
Fuga de agua	Leak
Grava	aggregate
Grava fina	fine aggregate
Grietas	cracks
pendiente del tejado	pitch (of a roof)
Interruptor	light switch
Hiladas	stretchers
Hilada de ladrillos	brick course
Hormigonera	concrete mixer
Hormigón	concrete
Humedad	dampness

ICP	miniature circuit breakers	*Radial*	circular saw
		Raedera	mattock
Impermeable	waterproof	*Reforzado*	underpinning
Interruptor	light switch	*Regla*	staight edge
Junta de compresión	compression fitting	*Regola*	chase
		Regulador de presión	pressure regulator
Ladrillos	bricks		
Lecheo	grout	*Rejas*	window bars
Lecheo	pointing	*Repisa*	shelf
Licencia de obras	planning permit	*Rosca de $^1/_2$ pulgada*	half-inch thread
Madera limpia	planed lumber		
Losas de barro	terracota tiles	*Ruina*	ruin
Macarrón	conduit	*Rústico*	rustic, rough
Mallazo	reinforcing mesh	*Saneamiento*	sewer line
		Sierra	saw
Masilla	putty lime	*Sequeta*	saw, for metal
Marco de la puerta	door frame	*Serrucho*	saw, for wood
Martillo	hammer	*Subvención*	grant
Mazo	sledge hammer	*Zuncho*	ring beam
Nivel	spirit level	*Soporte de canalón*	gutter bracket
Pago de transporte	delivery charge	*Tejado caído*	sagging roof
Pala	shovel	*Tejas de canal*	gutter tile
Palustra catalana	trowel	*Tejas superiores*	roof tiles (top)
Palustre	scraper, flat	*Tenazas*	pincers
Palustre de lengua de vaca	scraper, triangular	*Terminación tosca*	roughcast wall finish
Pared de tapia	stone and clay wall	*Tornillo cabeza redonda*	coachbolt
Peldaño	tread (of steps)	*Tornillo para madera*	countersunk screw
Pico	pickaxe		
Pintura	paint	*Traba*	wall tie
Pintura a la cal	limewash paint	*Tubo de cobre*	copper pipe
		Tubería de desagüe	waste pipe
Plana	float	*Turbina*	ventilator
Pozo séptico	septic tank	*Viga*	beam
Presupuesto	estimate	*Yeso*	plaster
Puntal	acro prop		

INDEX

For a free catalogue of all our books on Spain contact:
Santana Books
Apartado 422
29640 Fuengirola (Málaga).
Phone 952 485 838
Fax 952 485 367
Email: sales@santanabooks.com
www.santanabooks.com

UK Representatives
Aldington Books Ltd.
Unit 3(b) Frith Business Centre
Frith Road, Aldington
Ashford, Kent TN25 7HJ.
Tel: 01233 720 123. Fax: 01233 721 272
E-mail: sales@aldingtonbooks.co.uk
www.aldingtonbooks.co.uk